# INFESTED

END WORKPLACE DRAMA, STOP TOXIC EMPLOYEES, BUILD A THRIVING SMALL BUSINESS

## TIM WHITT

Infested: End Workplace Drama, Stop Toxic Employees, Build a Thriving Small Business

Written by Tim Whitt



Design and cover art by Peaceful Profits.

Paperback ISBN: 978-1-971949-06-2
eBook ISBN: 978-1-971949-07-9
Hardcover ISBN: 978-1-971949-08-6

# TABLE OF CONTENTS

*I didn't build this life by myself—not even close. God carried me through seasons I couldn't have survived on grit alone, and He put the right people in my path to keep me steady when I would've drifted, and to push me when I would've settled.*

*This is for the ones who held the line, paid the price, and helped make me the man behind these pages.*

# INTRO

I've been in the pest control industry for 45 years. I spent 30 years working for someone else, and for the last 15 years, I've run my own business, Pied Piper Pest & Lawn. That's not the route everyone would take, but I think I planned it well, because I could apply 30 years of experience and learning to Pied Piper from day one. And, wow, there was a lot of learning.

Obviously, the pest control industry is quite technical, so I experienced a serious practical, skills-based learning curve, but I learned a lot about business and management as well. And here's where it gets weird. There are so many parallels. I realized that I could apply the same thought processes and strategies to dealing with staff, clients, and suppliers that I used for assessing and controlling pest infestations in homes and offices. That may sound a bit off-the-wall but hear me out.

The first lesson I learned is that business is all about people—clients, employees, and suppliers. Once you've got them all working together in harmony, everything else falls into place. And then I had this crazy idea—people are just like pests. No, that sounds awful; only *some* people are like pests. And even that isn't really true. It's just that, sometimes, when you carefully analyze people's behavior, it really seems that they can behave a lot like cockroaches, fleas, rats, raccoons, flies, or pigeons. I thought about it for a while and realized that's because people have basically the same needs as all animals; so yes, people are like pests. But, perhaps more importantly, pests are like people. If you understand one, you can understand the other, because, quite honestly, we all want the same things: food, water, a safe place to live and bring up our children, and to be part of a community.

So I'm writing this book for anyone looking to start or grow a service-based business who knows that success depends not just on technical expertise, but on managing people—staff, clients, suppliers, and the broader community. I'll draw on my experiences both in the field and in the office to help you understand what makes service businesses run smoothly and how to keep them running smoothly. So whether you're just dreaming about running your own service business, are ready to take the first step, or are already in the thick of your business, I hope you'll find some useful information in these pages. And you'll also find some handy tips about pest control because I never stop thinking about those pesky critters. Some are scary, some are dangerous, some are devious, some cause immense damage, some can make you sick, and some can even kill you. But they're not bad; they're just animals living in a world that has changed a bit from the one they evolved in, so they're doing their best to survive. As are we all. The pests I encounter are just like people, and they behave just like people. Love them or hate them, you have to respect these resilient bugs and beasts that share our homes and business premises with us. The same goes for pesky humans, but that doesn't mean you have to put up with their disruptive behavior. I learned that in the corporate environment, and I carried it through to my own business.

## Taking That Big Step

When I began my career in the pest control industry, I had no plans to start my own business. I was 18 and I just wanted a regular paycheck. I stayed in pest control because the job allowed me to provide for my wife and the children we would eventually have. However, after a few years, I saw how fast the industry was growing and knew that it would not only be an excellent career path for me, but it could also provide me with the opportunity to build something for myself.

Back then, I didn't know that the challenges I faced in that job would teach me some of the most important lessons of all, especially about managing people. In my 30 years in a large corporate pest control company, I worked in every role within the organization. I started as a service technician and moved into sales and eventually into management, gaining firsthand experience with nearly every aspect of running a business that an owner is likely to face. Not only did I learn the ins and outs of the pest control industry, I learned how to work with and manage people.

Then, once my kids were grown, I made the move and started my own company, capitalizing on my experience in corporate. Once I made the decision to do it, I didn't look back. Over the past 15 years of running Pied Piper, I've been fortunate to see the business grow steadily. And I have no doubt that's because we've focused on doing right by our customers, which has led to a 4.9-star rating and more than 750 reviews on Google. In fact, almost all our clients come from referrals, and we spend practically nothing on marketing. That kind of growth didn't happen by accident; it came from applying the lessons I learned in the corporate world to every part of my business.

## Knowledge Is Power

In the 40-plus years I've been working in pest control, I've learned a lot about roaches, fleas, bedbugs, rats, and other vermin. And that's because knowledge is power. Say, for example, you see a rat or a roach in your home. You can buy a trap, rat poison, or spray from the store and use it, shotgun-style, to eliminate the unwelcome visitors. And it may work, or it may not. That's the problem with the shotgun approach.

That's why, as a pest control professional, I make a point of knowing and understanding how these critters live, love, and survive. Once I know their habits, I know where to find them and how to get rid of them. So, as I've stated, I've learned a lot over the years, but it's not all to do with creepy crawlies and nasty night visitors.

Slowly, I started to realize that managing people in business is just like managing pests. And, no, I haven't poisoned any of my employees, and I haven't stomped on any either. But I have relocated a few, because I worked out that they would be better suited to a different environment and—more importantly from my perspective—my environment would be much better off without people who behave the way they do. So I set them free in the wild, like I would a raccoon that had invaded someone's house.

It was just a twinkling of an idea at first, but once I started to notice that some people behave like problem animals, I couldn't let go of the idea. So I thought, what if I could work out how to deal with people by comparing them to insects, birds, and other critters? But management is not just about getting rid of workers who aren't contributing; it's more about creating an atmosphere in which employees can thrive, produce their best work, and contribute meaningfully to the company's bottom line. I also wondered whether I could learn how to motivate staff by considering how they resemble insects. And the answer is—yes!

We can learn a lot about management by watching how animals interact with their environment. We can use those lessons to ensure that our workplaces function optimally or, to take the analogy further, function like a healthy ecosystem with checks and balances.

In Part 1, I describe the actual animal pests and explain how to deal with them before moving on to their human counterparts. Part 2 is a structured outline of how to build and maintain a sustainable serviced-based business, using the principles in Part 1.

## Balance is Everything

As almost every eighth grader can tell you, a healthy ecosystem is one in which plants, animals, and microorganisms live together in harmony. The plants use sunlight to produce energy to fuel growth, and animals and microorganisms eat the plants to fuel their own growth. The amount of sunlight, soil, and water limits plant growth, which in turn, limits how many herbivores can eat those plants, and that determines how many predators can eat those animals. All these organisms die, and the energy tied up in their bodies returns to the ecosystem by being broken down by microorganisms, thereby increasing soil fertility and enabling more plants to grow. And then the cycle continues repeating.

However, if the system is out of balance, this beautiful symmetry breaks down. If there are too many predators, they'll eat up all the prey species and then starve. If there are too many herbivores, and not enough predators, they will eat up all the plants, and then they'll starve. That's a bit simplistic, but it's basically how it works. And businesses work the same way.

A business needs input the way a plant needs light, water, and air, so the procurement department ensures there is sufficient stock, raw materials, supplies, and/or infrastructure. Properly trained staff offer that stock for sale or utilize those raw materials and supplies to create value. Customers then purchase the stock, manufactured goods, or services by exchanging them for money, and that money goes to purchase more stock, raw materials, supplies, and/or infrastructure. Just like the ecosystem described above, this is a very simplified version of the truth, but it's pretty much what happens.

And, just like in the ecosystem, if there is an imbalance, the company will suffer. If, for example, there is insufficient stock or raw materials, the business cannot make sales, and if they don't make sales, they have no income. If they have no income, they can't pay their staff or their suppliers, and the system breaks down. Just like in the ecosystem, this value chain can be broken at almost any point for almost any reason.

And one of those reasons could be a person (staff member, client, supplier, or even management) who is behaving like a pest. Perhaps they are draining the company of resources like a bloodsucking mosquito, bedbug, or tick, or maybe they're vandals and saboteurs destroying the integrity of organizations by undermining the company like termites, flies, ants, pigeons, or spiders. Some pesky employees may even be stealing from the company like sneaky rats or scurrying cockroaches, and some may be active aggressors like wasps and scorpions, who attack the organization or other employees. Some suppliers, clients, or competitors may even squeeze the life out of a company just like one of those invasive Burmese pythons that have taken over the Florida Everglades. But it's not all bad; some pests demonstrate qualities we should imitate.

## The Good, The Bad, And The Ugly

We've been socialized into thinking only bad things about cockroaches, fleas, ticks, rats, raccoons, and other pests, but they are not innately bad. Just like most weeds are beautiful plants in the wrong place, most pests are not evil; they just happen to be in the wrong place.

We've learned to hate these creatures we call pests and to think of them as ugly and dirty, but they're really just perfectly evolved creatures competing for space in our environment. We resent them and, yes, if we want to maintain our standard of living, we need to find a way to deal with them. But it's not all negative. Bees, for example, are absolutely essential for our continued survival on this planet, but you don't want them in your living room. (And they wouldn't really be happy there, either.)

We consider most pests to be bad, but they have some good qualities, and ugliness is subjective. Other rats think big, tough rats with long, pointy tails are beautiful, and cockroaches admire the ones who have the shiniest carapaces and the most energetically wiggly antennae. Or at least, I suppose they do.

And, certainly, some so-called pests have many good qualities that we don't see because we are so focused on the negative. We can learn a lot about resilience from cockroaches, about lateral thinking and creativity from rats, about strategy from bedbugs, about hard work from ants, and about determination from fleas and ticks. So, while I've spent virtually all my working life in pest control, I understand that control is just that. It's not elimination; it's learning to find the balance.

In the following chapters, I'll introduce you to a range of pests and explain how they live, the type and level of threat they pose, and how we can safely and successfully manage them. I'll then outline how managers and business owners can use this same thought process to identify and control problematic people in their organizations and ecosystems to create and/or maintain a balanced business ecosystem.

And, importantly, I'll help you to recognize that, while you're carefully considering who in your staff or value chain might be the problem person, you need to occasionally glance at the mirror. In the same way that some pests, like roaches and rats, thrive in dirty, badly maintained homes, challenging staff often thrive in an environment with problematic management, and unruly clients and suppliers take advantage of dodgy business strategies, vague contracts, and irregular accounting practices. So always bear in mind that the problem person creating havoc in your organization might be you. One thing that pest control and management have in common is the need to keep an open mind, to judge situations on what is actually there, not what you hope might be there, believe should be there, or think might be there because you heard a rumor. In the pest control business, and in management, it is essential to base decisions on real, verified data.

Now, in the classic spaghetti Western alluded to in the heading above, the Clint Eastwood character is a bit like a pest control operative who arrives at the troubled premises, does some hardcore extermination, and then rides off into the sunset with a fistful of dollars. But that trope doesn't work for managers, and it doesn't really work for pest control companies either. As a manager, you are a part of the community, and you're in it for the long haul. Similarly, just like all other service providers, pest control companies thrive on repeat business. And you only get repeat business if you offer a well-thought-out, appropriate solution for each individual client; you're also in it for the long haul.

Unlike the steely-eyed poncho-wearing gunslinger, you need to deal with the fallout of your style of pest control and/or management; you should think long and hard before pulling out the spray gun—real or metaphorical. This is not the movies; we're talking about real life here. So let's have a look at some people-pests you might encounter in your business and how to manage them ethically and sustainably so your business can thrive and grow.

# PART 1

## A Pest-People Bestiary

Whether you're dealing with actual, physical, nonhuman pests out in the real world, or pest-like humans in your work environment, understanding is the key to management. Once you know what motivates them, what they're scared of, and what their kryptonite is, you can manage them and make your world a better place.

I've divided the most common pests into four major types: bloodsuckers, raiders, saboteurs and assailants. It's not a real scientific classification by any stretch of the imagination, but it works for me.

# CHAPTER 1

# Bloodsuckers—Vampires And Dementors Draining The Life Out Of People And Organizations

Vampires have been portrayed in so many different ways in literature, film, and media, that it's hard to know what to believe. From the soul-devouring dementors of the *Harry Potter* series to the erotic and bizarrely ethical vampires in the *Twilight* series, these mythological creatures are shown as evil, noble, pathetic, insane, terrifying, powerful, helpless, and genuinely funny. So, really, it's easy to know what to believe. None of it. Vampires are not real. But there are people who behave like vampires and dementors, and there are also bugs and insects that behave like vampires and genuinely do suck the blood from humans.

These are the bed bugs, fleas, ticks, and mosquitoes that feed on the blood of humans and animals. They don't (usually) kill their hosts, but they can. Most just debilitate their prey leaving them tired, lacking in energy and drive, and completely freaked out that some horrible little creature has invaded their space and—literally—drank their blood.

These real bloodsuckers all have a similar effect, but they require different treatment methods and chemical selections based on their differing habitats, lifestyles, and life cycles. In the same way, dealing with the metaphorical bloodsuckers also requires a different process depending on their strategy. So let's have a look at how the real bloodsucking pests operate and then apply that knowledge to dealing with their human counterparts.

## Stealth Muggers: Bedbugs

As a pest control professional, I can tell you that my most distressed clients are those who are plagued with bedbugs. These decidedly unloved beasties invade our most private spaces, our bedrooms. Where we should feel safe, where we can rest, where we retreat to recover from disease or injury, and where we can be vulnerable with our partners. Our sanctuaries.

Bedbugs are nocturnal parasites that feed on blood while their host sleeps, and most people don't even know they're there. They hide in tight cracks and can survive months without a meal. Their main weapon is stealth, so they are rarely seen. The only evidence of their existence is the mysterious appearance of irritating bites, and sometimes, a blood smear on the sheets that appears if you accidentally roll over on one during the night and crush it, releasing all the blood it sucked from you. So although you don't feel the bite, knowing that they are in your home, in your love-nest, and have been crawling over your body, is psychologically devastating.

However, while they're most commonly found in beds, and even named after them, they're decidedly sneaky, so you may find them in many other places. They love secondhand furniture and, if they get half a chance, they'll colonize your couch or favorite recliner. They are very good travelers, so they lurk in seedy hotels (and even some very smart hotels) just waiting for an opportunity to jump in your suitcase, so they can travel the world with you, and take up residence in your car, your home, and perhaps even your office. And, just when you thought it was safe to fly again, they absolutely love hanging out in the overhead compartment on planes. It's dark and cozy, so on long flights, they get to explore and choose a nice suitcase that will get them into a cab to a nice suburb where they can settle into a nice suburban home. Until they're discovered, and that's when I get the distress call.

## Critter Control—Helpful Tips

Prevention is always better than cure, so it's worth taking some precautions to ensure that you don't bring home unwelcome stowaways from your next vacation or business trip. When you get to a hotel, check the room for bedbugs. They are good at hiding, but they're not that hard to see if you know where to look. Use a bright flashlight and check all the likely spots. Of course, you'll pull back the sheets and check the bed, but don't stop there. They often hide behind the headboard, behind pictures on the wall, in the night stand, and even in the curtain rods—anywhere within 10 to 15 feet of the bed.

A simple way to prevent them from hopping into your luggage is to not use the closet, keep all your clothes in your bag, and keep your bag inside a sealed plastic bag. A bin liner will do; just make sure to tie it up tight. You could also keep your bag in the bathtub or shower as bedbugs are less likely to hide there.

Another way bedbugs sneak into houses is in secondhand furniture. If you buy used furniture, examine it carefully, and have it professionally steam cleaned. If it is free, buyer beware. You're getting what you paid for, and perhaps something extra. Also, consider carefully checking your child's room after sleepovers. Bedbugs can arrive in backpacks, pillows, and sleeping bags.

If you are unlucky enough to find the nasty critters in your home, don't panic. If it's just a few bugs that have managed to sneak in, you might be able to deal with it yourself. Vacuum them up, seal the vacuum bag and dispose of it far from the house. Pay particular attention to seams and cracks, and also vacuum under furniture. Wash all bedding and loose covers at a high heat, and dry in full sun or on high heat in a dryer. End off by steamcleaning the offended furniture, and your home should be free of the horrible little beasties. If it's more than just a few, or you just can't face dealing with it yourself, call an expert. You will be amazed how often we get called to the nicest, cleanest homes to deal with bedbugs. It's not an indictment of your housekeeping; it's just something that happens. Bad things can happen to good people.

## Business Analogy

Bedbug-like human bloodsuckers are usually not in your organization, so you sometimes don't even know they exist. They could be vendors overcharging, unnecessary intermediaries or agents, or even clients expecting unrealistic concessions. They may also be employees who are deliberately undermining your organization for some nefarious reason. Perhaps industrial espionage, or someone poaching clients for a rival firm. Wherever they lurk in your value stream, these nasty little critters siphon physical, intellectual, and/or financial assets from your business, weakening it in the process.

Failure to eradicate these "bedbug" personalities leads to slow internal decay, so early detection and direct confrontation are key.

In the same way that you would carefully check the room in an unknown hotel, you need to check every element that connects with your organization. Frequent check-ins expose silent saboteurs early, so create a culture of transparency. Check every new employee, vendor, agent, or client. Metaphorically pull back the sheets and look! What that means is check references; don't take resumes at face value, but follow up with previous employers and academic institutions to check that the accountant you're about to employ really does have a degree in finance. And always check their social media for tell-tale "smears" that indicate something is missing or at least not where it should be. You have to make every attempt, but it can be tricky because they are good at hiding.

Prevention is better than elimination, so work strictly to process and protocol. Make sure that all correspondence is properly filed, all decisions are properly minuted and filed, and—most important—all transactions are properly documented with orders, invoices, and receipts. It's the equivalent of taking a flashlight to the curtain rods in a hotel room.

## Learning From Experience

Back when I was running corporate operations at one of my busier locations, we brought on a customer service rep - let's call her Janet. On paper, she was a dream hire—years of experience, a sweet demeanor, and a Rolodex of contacts she hinted could "help us grow." She showed up early, kept her desk tidy, and never made a scene.

For months, she blended right in. The sales team liked her because she never argued about scheduling, and clients praised her "warm personality" on feedback calls. But slowly, something didn't add up.

Long-term accounts that had been stable for years started cancelling out of the blue. Always politely. Always without a complaint we could address. And curiously, they never came back.

We brushed it off at first. Clients change vendors all the time. But then one of our techs happened to be chatting with a former client who let slip that they were now using a smaller, newer company that "Janet recommended." I connected the dots pretty quickly after that.

Janet was the perfect bedbug—quiet, out of sight, working where you'd never think to look, but draining value night after night. She was passing existing customer pricing information and service protocol along with new leads to a friend's company for a kickback.

**The Lesson:** Just like a bedbug hides deep in the seams of a mattress or behind a painting where you'd never think to look, saboteurs hide in the folds of your business process. So, it's a good idea to periodically "pull back the sheets" on client churn. Look at the data, ask exit questions, and track where they're going. Early detection saves you from slow, invisible decay.

## Tenacious Freeloaders: Fleas And Ticks

Fleas and ticks are external parasites that attach to hosts for prolonged feeding and can go unnoticed for days. Flea bites and tick bites are irritating and itchy, but are usually not serious. However, they can and sometimes do transmit disease. In the US, ticks carry a number of diseases including Lyme disease, which can result in long-term chronic disability, and ticks in other parts of the world can transmit similar nasty infections. Fleas can carry a range of microbes that can cause diseases ranging from mild fevers to the deadly—but rare— bubonic plague.

### Critter Control—Helpful Tips

Fleas live on a number of furry animals, including dogs, cats, mice, and rats, and they also live in houses, especially carpets, furniture, and pet beds, where they may go unnoticed for a while. And, while they don't usually live on people, they'll happily hop on for a quick blood meal.

Fleas have an interesting life cycle. One female flea can lay 50 eggs per day, and many of these fall off the host animal, landing on the carpet, bed, couch, or wherever Fluffy or Fido likes to hang out. The eggs then hatch into larvae, which wander around undetected eating all sorts of very tiny, disgusting stuff like flea poop, bits of dead skin, and even tiny bits of dead fleas. Tasty, right? After they've eaten enough of this stuff to grow into a flea, they wrap themselves in a cocoon that will protect them from excessive heat, cold, or dryness, and even insecticide. Fleas, or at least flea pupae in cocoons, are patient. They'll hang around until they detect a full-blooded animal walking past and will then immediately emerge, clamber up onto the ambulatory larder, and start feeding.

This is why empty houses can be so flea-infested. If all the warm, delicious humans and pets leave a house to go on vacation, the flea eggs continue to hatch, the larvae have plenty of food, so they continue to grow, and then they pupate. And then they wait, and while they're waiting, even more larvae hatch and feed and pupate.

And then, unsuspectingly, you walk in the door, and before you are halfway across the living room, you have fleas up to your knees. You can try to deal with this using store-bought insecticide, which might make a dent, but this could be the time to call in the big guns. I can't tell you how many traumatized people have phoned me minutes after returning from vacation.

The best way to deal with this issue is, of course, prevention. If you have pets, take them to the vet regularly for tick and flea prophylaxis; there are some great over-the-counter products as well. Even if you do that, be proactive about de-fleaing your home if you're going to be away for a few weeks and you suspect a problem may arise. If you even suspect there may be one or two fleas in your home, vacuum and steam clean all carpets and furniture, and wash all pet bedding at high temperatures and dry in full sun or high heat in the dryer.

Ticks live out in the woods and grasslands, where they can spend days or even weeks clinging to leaves or grass, waiting for an unsuspecting deer, raccoon, dog, cow, other animal, or even human to brush past and provide a yummy blood meal. They have a similar life cycle to fleas, but unlike fleas, they need to eat blood at every stage. They are "faithful" to one host per stage, but they usually find a new host for the next stage. So, it's unlikely that you will find ticks living independently in your home the way fleas do.

The best way to avoid picking up these freeloading hitchhikers is to wear insect repellent when out hiking, paying particular attention to your legs and feet, but not ignoring the rest of you. They are most often found in grass, but may also be in the trees above or beside you.

## Business Analogy

Parasitic in nature, tick- and flea-like humans latch on for personal gain and are hard to remove. They are the freeloaders and opportunists who attach themselves to others' success and suck resources without reciprocation. They may, for example, enjoy the benefits of belonging to a high-performing department without actually contributing to their team's success. This, in turn, can demotivate the more hardworking team members until, like the victims of J.K. Rowling's dementors, they have become soulless husks that wander aimlessly around the office, staring into the middle distance, to the ultimate detriment of the whole team and the company.

As with the real ticks and fleas, the best way to deal with these parasitic employees is through good hygiene, or more precisely, proper process. Healthy boundaries and performance metrics are the repellent here. Define contribution standards clearly and document performance to prevent long-term parasitism. Over-accommodating poor performers creates imbalance and resentment.

Another way that "bloodsucking" parasites can drain resources from a company is by creating unnecessary intermediaries. This problem tends to be more common in very small or very large businesses. Small business owners or emerging entrepreneurs may believe conniving agents and representatives that they would not be able to access markets without them, so they willingly—but reluctantly—hand over a percentage of their income as commission, agent's fees, management fees, or finder's fees. Perhaps even more pernicious are the procurement managers in large organizations who buy supplies or services from their friends or family who do not actually produce the required goods but acquire it from a third party and just add on a percentage—some of which will, of course, go back to the procurement officer one way or another. Guard against this by creating and maintaining a transparent and squeaky-clean supply chain, with each and every supplier and customer verified.

As with fleas that thrive in homes where the vacuum cleaner remains in the broom closet from week to week, intermediary parasites thrive in companies with questionable standards. For example, not keeping clear records may be due to sheer laziness, or it may even be a deliberate strategy to fudge payments, avoid tax, or even deliberately underpay suppliers or overcharge customers. Such questionable business morals leave business owners and managers open to falling victim to the same strategies from their employees who, rightly, can shrug their shoulders and say, "Well, if the company does it, why shouldn't I?"

And, taking the flea analogy a bit further, do not ignore tiny infringements by just one person. Like the poop-eating larvae lurking in your household carpet, if left unattended, small infractions can grow exponentially and, before you know it, you're up to your metaphorical knees in metaphorical fleas, and the company's cash flow has become an uncontrolled arterial hemorrhage.

**Learning From Experience**

When I was managing a busy corporate branch, I had a tech named (for the purpose of this book) Alan. He appeared to have a steady hand—rarely made waves and got along with everyone, and his numbers always looked solid. What made him stand out was the size of his commission checks. Month after month, they were higher than what most mid-level techs could dream of.

At first, I chalked it up to him "figuring something out." But the more I looked at his sales records, the stranger it seemed. Alan's name kept appearing on big-ticket jobs that originated in the office, not in the field.

One day, a routine internal audit turned into something more. While reviewing a particularly large sale, I noticed the timeline didn't match. The job had been booked by a customer service rep (let's call her Paula)—no field inspection, no proposal logged—but Alan was listed as the salesperson. That didn't make sense.

I started quietly asking questions, and the truth eventually trickled out from a couple of sharp-eyed coworkers. Alan had a side arrangement with Paula. When high-value leads came into the office, Paula would "assign" them to Alan, bypassing other sales reps. Alan would run the appointment, close the sale—often with minimal effort since the client was already ready to buy—and then, once the commission check hit, he'd split it with Paula under the table.

It was a perfect flea-and-tick partnership. Paula fed him the host. Alan latched on, took his fill, and then shared the blood meal. The company paid for both bites—once to Alan in commission and again in lost opportunities for the sales reps who should have gotten those leads.

The damage wasn't just financial. Word got around, as it always does. The hunters (sales reps) in my team started to lose faith in the fairness of the system. And when hunters stop hunting, the whole ecosystem suffers, and some of them might leave for more productive hunting grounds.

After we uncovered their scheme, Alan and Paula were shown the door. But the real fix was tightening the system. We put controls in place; leads were assigned by sales territory and zip code, commissions were audited monthly, and customer files had to show a full trail from contact to close. Just like ticks, freeloaders cling until you pull them off with tweezers. The best defense is strong processes that don't leave room for them to latch on.

**The Lesson:** Fleas and ticks don't work alone—they often thrive in pairs and groups. In business, that's the dangerous alliance between a frontline opportunist and an inside enabler. The only defense is transparency. Assign sales territories to track the source of every sale, and make sure commissions are tied to documented effort; because if you let these partnerships feed unchecked, they'll drain your best people and poison your culture.

## Noisy Nuisances or Silent Assassins: Mosquitoes

Mosquitoes are small, insignificant insects that eat nectar and pollinate plants. That's true, but it's not the whole truth. Yes, they are small, but they could be considered very significant in terms of their effect. Responsible for close to a million deaths annually, mosquitoes are the most dangerous nonhuman animal on the planet. Snakes come in a sluggish second with less than 200,000 deaths a year. Of course, mosquitoes don't bludgeon their victims to death, and they don't eat them. They kill them by transmitting deadly diseases such as malaria, dengue fever, Zika virus, West Nile fever, yellow fever, and various forms of encephalitis. We can all agree that their incessant buzzing keeps people awake and can drive even the mildest-mannered person totally crazy.

The bit about living on nectar is also true. Mosquitoes (male ones, anyway) are vegetarian. And so are female mosquitoes, at least until they start thinking about babies, because they need a protein boost to lay eggs, and the only way they can get it is through fresh blood. So, a broody female mosquito will sneak up on an unsuspecting animal or human, stab them with her incredibly sharp proboscis, and start sucking. Once she's had her meal, she leaves. But she also leaves behind a bit of saliva, which may or may not contain a virus or a host of other microorganisms. Some of these are harmless, but others are not. Among the most dangerous is the malaria plasmodium—the invisible, squishy, single-celled creature responsible for the deaths of hundreds of thousands of children every year, along with many adults.

As a rule in the US, mosquitoes are more of a nuisance than a threat, and a bite from one will result in nothing more than an irritating itchy spot. However, according to the Centers for Disease Control and Prevention (CDC), they can transmit a range of viral infections, some of which are very serious. And, just to make them even more sinister, anopheles mosquitoes—the really dangerous ones—don't buzz. Like ninjas, they are silent but deadly.

## Critter Control—Helpful Tips

There are two ways of dealing with mosquitoes: reducing the places where they can breed and keeping them as far away from you as possible. Mosquitoes need open water to breed, but it doesn't have to be a lake. An ornamental pond, blocked gutters, or old tires lying around in the yard are all perfect places for mosquito larvae to swim around until they're ready to get their wings. However, try as you may, you are unlikely to completely eradicate them from your immediate environment. You can keep them out of your house by fitting screens to your windows and, if you're outside, you can keep them away from you by using repellent. If you're sitting on the patio, try a fan with adjustable speeds. It's also a good idea to wear long sleeves and long pants in the evening, which can be irritating in summer, but it's one of the best ways of keeping these annoying bloodsuckers at bay.

## Business Analogy

Just like real mosquitoes, mosquito-like human pests in the business environment may be just irritating, or they may constitute a serious threat; it's hard to tell which it is. Like all bloodsuckers, they take without giving, but these pesty people tend to take attention, time, and energy. These are the chronic interrupters, needy people, or attention seekers who waste time by pulling leaders from higher priorities, derailing meetings, and constantly injecting drama to stay relevant. They home in on attention, hog everyone's time, energy, and focus, and contribute nothing but irritation. Pay close attention; they really are drawn to calm waters only to breed, overpopulate, and take control.

Like dealing with the nasty little insects, the best way to deal with these energy vampires is to put up screens or wear some repellent to keep them at a safe distance. Define processes for meetings and put gatekeepers or buffers in place to keep time-wasters out of your office. Of course, that only works if the time-wasting bloodsucker is lower on the management ladder. Protecting employees who report to the time bandit may be trickier. You may have to do some yard redecorating by removing whatever it is that makes it possible for them to exist and multiply. We're obviously not talking about old tires or blocked gutters, but simply moving the furniture may create enough space to change the dynamic.

## Learning From Experience

Stealing time and energy is subtle and sometimes hard to detect, so making a fuss about it may seem a bit petty. But wasting time is a form of theft that should not be ignored because minor transgressions can lead to bigger ones. People who steal time may be stealing more concrete things too.

I had a senior tech I'll call Larry. Larry had been with us for years. He knew his routes like the back of his hand, had customers who swore by him, and could handle even the most stubborn pest situations without breaking a sweat. Out in the field, he was worth his weight in gold.

But once he stepped through the office door at the end of his route, his focus shifted—and not in a good way. He had a knack for turning a simple end-of-day check-in into a full-scale social event.

It would start innocently enough. He'd pop into the breakroom to drop off his paperwork or refill his coffee mug. Then he'd launch into a story—maybe about a customer who swore they'd seen a mouse the size of a small dog or about the time he climbed into an attic only to come nose-to-nose with a raccoon who wasn't in the mood for visitors.

Larry was a natural storyteller. He had timing, expression, and just enough embellishment to make you forget about the pile of work on your desk. People would start drifting in— first one tech, then a customer service rep, then another tech who "just needed to grab something," but ended up leaning on the doorframe listening. Before long, half the staff was there, laughing, swapping their own stories, and losing track of time.

This was the Pied Piper paradox: In a large corporation, Larry's antics might have been an amusing end-of-day distraction— annoying, but contained. In a small business like mine, where there were only five people in the office, it was dangerous. If two or three of them were standing in the breakroom instead of working, it wasn't just a little slowdown—it was a productivity hemorrhage.

And it wasn't just about lost time. The "Larry Breakroom Effect" changed the energy of the day. That post-route downtime bled into the next task, and before long, instead of wrapping up paperwork, making follow-up calls, or preparing for the next day, people were coasting toward quitting time. One mosquito bite isn't fatal—but enough of them, day after day, will wear you down, especially if they're accompanied by an irritating whine. And, while even I have to agree Larry's stories were great, they definitely started to sound like an irritating whine when I realized what they were costing the business.

So I had to step in. We talked about the importance of staying focused during office hours, about how those last 30 minutes of the day could make or break tomorrow's schedule. Larry wasn't malicious—he genuinely didn't see the ripple effect. But I made it clear: Stories were fine, just not during the workday. If he wanted to hold court, it could happen after hours, not on company time. In the end, it wasn't about shutting Larry down—it was about putting up a screen. Mosquitoes can't get through a net, and time-wasters can't thrive when you've got clear boundaries.

**The Lesson:** In a small business, mosquito-like time-wasters sting harder and leave a mark that lingers. You can't afford slow afternoons. Boundaries aren't optional—they're survival. Set office-hour expectations, cut off side conversations before they spiral, and keep the focus on moving the work forward. In a company where every role matters, protecting productivity is the same as protecting profit.

We've dealt with the types of humans and creatures that steal your blood, so now let's look at the ones that steal your stuff.

# CHAPTER 2

# Raiders—Bandits and Burglars Taking Without Giving

In almost every culture and religion, theft is wrong. However, different people define theft in different ways, and some people even define different types of theft. Some people consider Robin Hood-type thieving from the rich, and maybe even defrauding an insurance company that rips you off to be okay, but pickpocketing someone's wallet or burgling someone's home are almost universally considered bad. Using the company printer to print your kid's school project and taking stationery home from the office usually fall somewhere in between. But even "minor" theft has a cost for the victim, so where do you draw the line?

These are the cockroaches, rats, and raccoons that help themselves to whatever they need or want. Some are sneaky and secretive, some are clever opportunists, and some are brazen, but the one thing they have in common is that they enrich themselves at your expense. Also, they tend to negatively impact the environment until, eventually, living or working there becomes untenable, and you have to eradicate them or move. Their human counterparts steal both literally and figuratively from the organization, the individuals working there, and clients. However, it's not usually the loss of the stolen items that causes the damage, but rather the process and the very fact that you have a raider on your team.

All of these light-fingered invaders have a similar effect, but because the scale of their effects vary and because they use different strategies, they require different treatment methods. In the same way, dealing with the human raiders in your organizations also requires a different process depending on their strategy, so let's have a look at how the real thieving pests operate and then apply that knowledge to dealing with their human counterparts.

## Sneaky Scroungers (Roaches)

Almost no one likes cockroaches, but you have to admire their resilience and their superb strategy. Popular wisdom has it that the last remaining creatures on earth after a nuclear apocalypse will be cockroaches. This may be true because they can withstand extreme environments and are notoriously hard to kill. They certainly are the ultimate survivors.

They are nocturnal, so they come out at night to forage and will scatter back to their secret hidey-holes as soon as you turn on a light. Because they're not very big, you probably won't even notice what they steal, so making a fuss might seem petty.

However, it's not what they take that matters, but how they change your environment. Cockroaches, actually, are very clean, and are constantly grooming themselves, but they can and do carry diseases because they walk over and through all kinds of nasty things, like drains and sewers. They can leave various types of pathogens on the food they've barely made a dent in. You won't see this, of course, and you probably won't even make the connection, but it's worth thinking about if you pick up some otherwise inexplicable gastric infection. Also, just having cockroaches in your house could make you feel dirty, poor, uneducated, and just icky, and one single cockroach sighting in a restaurant is virtually a death knell.

## Critter Control—Helpful Tips

Cockroaches do very well in homes where dirty dishes are left on countertops with yummy food scraps they can snack on all night, but they can survive—even thrive—on barely visible food sources. Seriously, one unwashed knife can be a Thanksgiving dinner for a whole family of cockroaches. And it's not just the kitchen. If you eat in front of the TV or your kids eat in their bedrooms, there are likely to be crumbs all over the house. A real buffet—for bugs! So, either shape up and clean up real good, or accept that…you are not alone (creepy music optional).

But it's not worth getting upset about. Even the cleanest, most sanitary homes can be invaded by these clever critters. And some parts of some cities are so overrun with roaches, it's virtually impossible to completely eliminate them from your home. Here's a scary fact. One female cockroach, if stressed or dying, can drop an egg sac with anywhere between 10 and 50 eggs. They're almost invisible and are very hard to get rid of.

It's not just a matter of killing the critters; you need to dispose of the bodies and also find and dispose of the egg sacs. Fun fact: you need to dispose of the bodies because—yes—they are a food source for other cockroaches. And you thought cockroaches couldn't get more fun.

Your best strategy is to regularly employ a reputable pest control professional to prevent them from getting out of control. I recommend you do this no less than quarterly for homes and monthly for commercial premises. Bait gel and properly placed bait stations, or more poetically, roach motels, are relatively effective for small populations, but you need to make sure they are attractive by eliminating all competing food sources. Also, you have to constantly monitor them because empty roach motels are just that—motels. They make great nests.

## Business Analogy

Like their creepy crawly counterparts, human cockroach-pests are not actually harmful in themselves; they just make the office a less pleasant place to be in. But they do this so sneakily, it's hard to put your finger on it. Often, these are the well-entrenched people who've always been there, and nobody really knows what they do. They don't really contribute, and they definitely don't make a fuss, but you also can't seem to get rid of them. You'll usually find this type of pest when you take over a new division or even a new company. They are often the repositories of extensive institutional knowledge, so new managers don't feel comfortable firing them because the stuff they know isn't written down anywhere. They know where the bodies are buried! Once you've been running the department for a while, you may find that, just when you thought you could persuade them to leave, or even fire them, you find they've created another little power base or niche that makes it impossible to shift them.

And it's not just that they don't earn their keep and create no value. They create an atmosphere that other employees find difficult. Just like no one likes living with cockroaches roaming the halls, no one likes a colleague who does nothing but draws a salary anyway. They avoid accountability, hide mistakes, and cunningly manage to be gone when things go wrong.

And, like the real cockroaches, even once you've got rid of them, you have to do a lot of work to clean up after them. They're not likely to leave actual egg sacs, but you should carefully go through their files to check they have not initiated processes that can continue to do the organization harm.

As with real cockroaches, these pests do not like the light, so openness and transparency are the best tools for protecting yourself and your company. They thrive in the dark, scatter under pressure, and are incredibly resilient.

**Learning From Experience**

When I was a corporate service manager, I worked with a guy I'll call Carl who had been with the company seemingly forever. He wasn't loud, he wasn't aggressive, and superficially, he didn't seem like a problem. He was just…there. Always there.

But it didn't take long for me to realize Carl was the human version of a cockroach. He never did enough to get fired, but he also never did anything to actually pull his weight. His daily route sheets were always light, his production numbers barely acceptable, and yet, somehow, he survived year after year.

Here's how he operated. When equipment went missing, Carl was nowhere to be found. When a job went sideways, he was conveniently "off that account." When customers complained, he had an excuse ready—and senior management bought it every time. And yet, when the office handed out credit for good months, Carl was standing right there, smiling, blending in, acting like he'd earned it.

What frustrated me most wasn't Carl himself—it was the way senior management handled him. Instead of shining a light, they let him keep skittering around in the shadows. They told the rest of us to "pick up the slack" while Carl got a free pass. And just like with real cockroaches, it wasn't the one you saw that was the problem—it was what he represented. His presence sent the message that hiding, dodging, and doing the bare minimum was acceptable.

The real damage wasn't his lack of production. It was how he contaminated the culture. Other techs saw him get away with it and started thinking, "Why am I busting my back if Carl gets paid the same?" And that's how the infestation begins.

I tried talking to him and gave him a formal warning to enforce production standards, but he just kept getting sneakier. I shouldn't have been surprised because cockroaches don't change. After all, they are the ultimate survivors, so why mess with a winning formula? I had to fire him, but that wasn't the end of it. I also had to put a lot of work into fixing the damage he'd done to team morale.

**The Lesson:** Cockroaches remind us that survival isn't the same as progress. Businesses that protect these shadow dwellers may limp along, but they'll never thrive. If you want a thriving team, you can't let the cockroaches hide in the walls. You've got to rip out the drywall and fix what's behind it.

## The Ultimate Opportunists (Rats)

It's a toss-up which are the most hated home invaders, cockroaches or rats. Like cockroaches, rats don't actually take that much, but they can be so destructive, and they're scary. An adult rat can grow to about 11 inches—that's not including the tail—and can weigh over a pound. They are extremely intelligent, which is why they make good pets, but it's also why they make formidable rivals for living space. They can climb walls and can squeeze through the tiniest gaps. Like most animals (and humans) they require a cozy place to live that is warm, dry, and safe, and has a source of water and food. Some of their favorite spots are behind fridges, where it's warm, safe, and close to the kitchen for a foraging expedition once the humans have gone to bed. They also live in the walls, and they have been known to take up residence in the engine compartments of cars, possibly because of the plant base insulation and wiring harness on electrical wires. This is still a debated topic, but it seems they can smell the soy-based materials, so they can cause havoc by shorting out electric systems in your home or car and possibly even causing fires. So, yes, it's not what they steal, but the destruction they cause.

Also, rats are fussy eaters, so they won't just take one banana out of the fruit bowl; they'll sample them all to see which is the tastiest. And then you're left with six or seven inedible bananas because they have bite marks all over them and who knows what else. They also, obviously, have to defecate and urinate somewhere so, you guessed it: on your kitchen floor, on the kitchen counter, in your kitchen cabinets, and in your fruit bowl. Everywhere!

In warehouses and restaurants, they'll gnaw through bags to sample the contents and then leave four or five or ten broken—unsellable and unusable—bags lying around. And the next night, they'll try new bags rather than returning to the ones they've already accessed. Even in offices, the domino effect of one or two rats munching away at supplies and defecating behind the desks and filing cabinets—or enjoying the food snacks you left in the upper right hand drawer of your desk—is immense. It just makes the office a not-nice place to be. Both rats and mice can and do carry a range of diseases; while a few are not that serious, some, like hantavirus and bubonic plague, are deadly.

## Critter Control—Helpful Tips

As with most pests, preventing a rat infestation is better than needing to eradicate them; however, depending on where you live or do business, rats can be hard to keep out. In some of the older parts of cities, it's estimated there may be one rat for every four humans. They really are ubiquitous, so the best you can do is try to keep them out of your very small part of the world, which requires constant vigilance. The most important part of the strategy is to not leave food lying around. That includes pet food and, in suburban gardens, edible scraps in compost heaps. Once they've found their way into your home or business, though, you're best off calling in the big guns. A reputable pest control professional will not only remove them as humanely and effectively as possible, but will also help you identify how they got in and help you create a strategy for keeping them out in the future: as far as possible. Rats are frustratingly clever pests.

## Business Analogy

The lesson from rats and mice is that the visible damage may only be the tip of the metaphorical iceberg. One tiny hole in a bag of corn in a food warehouse is indicative of a bigger problem, and it also means you've lost a hundred pounds of corn. Tiny toothmarks on electrical cables may be barely noticeable but they can cause a fire that can burn down whole buildings and even kill people. As a manager, you need to disregard the size of the hole and concentrate on the possible downstream effect.

In an office, the occasional disappearance of a yogurt from the communal fridge may be considered to be just a nuisance, but it can negatively affect office culture and team spirit by instilling a sense of distrust. So, yes, it's not the size of the infraction; two yogurts a month is really no big deal, but not trusting your coworkers is a big deal.

In the same way, someone coming in to work five minutes late is also not really that serious. But if they do it every day, and other employees start doing the same, things can get out of hand. Five minutes becomes ten minutes, one late employee becomes two, becomes five, becomes ten, and before you know it, you're losing about two hours of productivity every single day. Add that up.

And it's not just the beginning of the day. Rats are notorious for being the first to leave a sinking ship, and your human rat-pest is likely to shave a few minutes off the end of the day too. Think of the person who leaves their desk 15 minutes before quitting time to go to the bathroom, where they'll do their hair, brush their teeth, fix their makeup, maybe even shave in preparation for a post-work date. And then, one minute to five, they're back at their desk, ostentatiously turning off their computer and walking out with everyone else.

Or they might religiously stay at their desk from nine to five, but spend much of that time on the phone with friends, doing their nails, doing the crossword, or blowing up social media. Rats are good at spotting even the tiniest gap, and they'll take it. Not only that, while they're sneaking through, they'll take a few bites to make it easier next time, so other ~~rats~~ employees will notice the now bigger hole and start sneaking through. Rats are social.

Dealing with these constant tiny infringements can be hard, which is why a good HR manager is so important. Ideally, you want to nip that kind of behavior in the bud. But if you can't persuade them to change their ratty ways, you may need to find a way to get rid of them. Not poison, obviously. Really, don't leave poisoned yogurts in the fridge.

**Learning From Experience**

Later in my corporate career, when I was running one of the busier branches, I had a technician I'll call Mike. On the surface, Mike looked like a superstar. His production was consistently high, his commission checks were some of the biggest in the office, and upper management loved to point to him as an example of success.

But something about his numbers didn't sit right with me. They were too good, too consistent, and always just a step above everyone else. I'd been around long enough to know when a rat had found a hole.

So I started watching him more closely.

What I found was exactly what I feared. Mike was cutting corners. He'd rush through jobs, skipping inspections and spraying just enough to make it look like the work was done. Customers thought they were covered, but a week later, they'd be calling back with the same problems. His callbacks were climbing, but he was slick about making sure someone else picked them up.

The rest of the team saw what was happening. They knew they were working harder, staying longer, and still taking home smaller checks than Mike. The resentment was palpable. One day, a tech came into my office and asked, "Why should I work so hard if Mike's going to get rewarded for taking shortcuts?" That was the moment it hit me—the damage wasn't just in the field. The real damage was in the culture.

When a rat gnaws a hole in a bag of grain, the loss isn't just the handful they eat; it's the hundreds of pounds contaminated by the opening. Mike's shortcuts weren't just hurting customers; they were eating away at the trust and morale of the entire team.

Once the truth was undeniable, I had to act. I sat down with Mike, laid out the pattern, and gave him a choice: Change your ways, or we'll find someone who will. He didn't change, and eventually, he was gone. It was the right call, but it left me with a leadership scar I've carried ever since.

**The Lesson:** Numbers alone lie. Rats often look like superstars until you shine a light on how they got those numbers. As a leader, you can't just celebrate production; you have to inspect it. Because if you reward the rat, you're not just feeding him. You're training the rest of the pack to chew holes in your business.

## Brazen Masked Bandits (Raccoons)

Unlike rats and cockroaches, raccoons are almost likeable at a distance when they're out in the woods. They're not so adorable when they knock over your bins and leave garbage strewn all over the place, and they are definitely not cute at all when they invade your house, empty your cupboards, and strew food and broken containers all over your kitchen. They also leave other unmentionable traces of their visit on their way out—disgusting! But raccoons don't enter homes only to steal food; they're also looking for shelter. Raccoons can make themselves very comfortable under and between floors and in roofs, crawl spaces, and even wall cavities.

These beasts get very big, with some adult males weighing in at over 50 pounds, and while they're not usually aggressive, they can bite. They can carry disease, including—extremely rarely—rabies.

## Critter Control—Helpful Tips

Keeping raccoons away is all about making your home unattractive to them. Do not leave food in unsecured bins overnight, and don't leave any food outside, including pet food. Close up any holes or gaps that may allow them to access warm, dark, unused spaces in your home, like between the ceiling and the roof, behind walls, and under floors.

If you've fallen victim to a raccoon home invasion, it's best to call a professional. They're big, clever, sneaky, sometimes hard to catch, and hard to handle once caught. Professionals would usually do a live capture and release them in the wild if state laws allow, and then carefully examine your home to find out how they're getting in. Raccoons are extremely bright. I've seen them open doors and windows, and even climb down chimneys like a sinister Santa Claus. They're problem solvers, so keeping them at bay requires constant vigilance.

## Business Analogy

Your raccoon-like person may—like the really rather cute raccoon—seem fabulous at first. Like their furry counterparts, they are strong-willed, clever, and determined. These are the clever workers who've found a loophole that allows them to shave a bit extra off each payment, a way to manipulate data to increase their commissions, or some other way or glitch to beat the system. And, like the cute, stripey-tailed counterparts, they're generous. They share their information and spoils with coworkers, which has one major advantage for them and a disadvantage for you. Sharing is a good way to encourage coworkers not to spill the beans.

They may also be sharing their loot with clients. These are the reps who collude with buyers from other companies to over-invoice and underdeliver, with the extra payment being evenly shared between the two. It's a double win for the rep, because they may even get commission on the misappropriated funds.

## Learning From Experience

The thing about raccoons is that they don't sneak around the way roaches or rats do. They're bold. They'll climb into your trash can in broad daylight, knock the lid off, and stare you down while they dig through your leftovers. That's what makes them so dangerous in business—raccoon-people aren't timid thieves. They're brazen. They know how to work the system, and they count on your silence or distraction to get away with it.

I've seen raccoons take many forms over the years.

There was the vendor who padded every invoice with "miscellaneous charges," hoping no one would notice. There was the sales rep who charmed clients into sweetheart deals while quietly slipping a little extra into his own pocket. And then there was the long-term employee who treated the company truck like his personal vehicle—running errands on the clock, putting weekend miles on it, and even filling it with supplies for side jobs that had nothing to do with us.

The scary part? They weren't hiding. They were doing it in plain sight, smiling while they did it. Like raccoons, they looked you in the eye while they made the mess, confident you'd be too busy or too polite to challenge them.

The temptation as an owner is to shrug off small thefts or cut corners because confronting them feels uncomfortable. But the lesson I've learned is that raccoons don't stop at scraps. Once they know the lid is loose, they'll tip the whole can over. And when that happens, it's not just the food they ruin; it's the environment around it. Trust erodes, honest employees get discouraged, and suddenly you're not running a business; you're cleaning up a campsite that's been raided.

**The Lesson:** Raccoon-people are brazen, clever, and generous enough to buy silence. But they only succeed when leaders let them. The real danger isn't their theft; it's your tolerance. The fix isn't just catching the raccoon. It's making sure the lids are locked, the trash isn't left out, and the message is clear: Daylight robbery isn't tolerated here.

These pests make life unpleasant for everyone else, and they decrease the efficiency and efficacy of companies and organizations even though they don't mean to. It's just the collateral damage of their thieving activities. But some pests don't even steal; they just make life hard for coworkers, employers, and clients by subtly or not-so-subtly destabilizing organizations and causing general mayhem. These are the vandals and villains who undermine processes and destroy the integrity of organizations and relationships.

# CHAPTER 3

# Saboteurs—Thugs and Hooligans That Destroy the Peace

Vandals destroy the infrastructure and ambience of the organization, and saboteurs disrupt the free flow of information and creativity. Both thrive on negative office politics, petty rivalries, and unkind gossip. Sometimes they benefit from the process but, more often, they're just destructive for no good reason, undermining the very structure of your business.

These human pests make life miserable, and so do their animal counterparts. Flies can drive you crazy with their constant buzzing, and they always seem to be in your face. Pigeons are just as bad, quietly cooing, gathering together, and leaving unmentionable deposits all over the driveway, your car, and any statue within range. Less obvious, but perhaps even more damaging, are the termites that quietly, slowly, and persistently demolish your home, office, or other infrastructure from the inside out, and the silverfish that lurk in the dark, destroying files and records. Also irritating are the busy-busy-busy ants always running around frantically and those sneaky, subtle spiders that spin a stupendous web and then just wait. And wait.

## The Noisy Nuisance (Buzzing Flies)

Just one fly can drive you crazy. It buzzes around your head, getting closer and closer, and then just when you grab a swatter to kill it, it settles…just out of reach. And, as you bring the swatter down, it does a vertical takeoff like an F-35B Lightning II jet and then dodges around the room doing impossible right-angled turns. They have a short lifespan, and they lay their eggs in garbage, feces, or decaying matter, like—yeah, disgusting—dead bodies. So they, literally, have $#1t on their shoes, and they bring it into your kitchen. They settle on your food, rubbing their little legs together to dislodge any garbage, rotting flesh, or fresh feces. Fun fact: A female house fly can lay up to 500 eggs in her short life, which is about 15 to 30 days on average.

### Critter Control—Helpful Tips

The secret to keeping your home or business a no-fly zone is hygiene and strategy. If there's nowhere nearby for them to breed, they're less likely to make it to your front door, and if your house is well screened, they're not likely to get in. But, of course, if you're running a business, you need to keep the doors open, literally and metaphorically. Back in the middle of the twentieth century, plastic, yellow fly strips did the trick, but that look just won't swing in the twenty-first century.

Flies literally stick to the fly strip hanging from a ceiling. Not only does it provide limited control, but a lot of health inspectors and consumers just don't want to see it. The real problem is that as the fly decays, it (and the fly strip) can fall and land on what's below - food or people!

Air curtains are more effective and certainly more aesthetic because they are totally and completely invisible. While flies can perform pretty spectacular aerial maneuvers, they can't fly against the wind, so all the air curtain has to do is maintain a constant airflow that the fly simply cannot cross.

Depending on where you are, flies may be more problematic. If you're on a farm, for example, you'll need to be a bit more proactive and may need to use fly baits and properly placed traps or install an automatic spray system. If you're dealing with more than a few nuisance flies, you'll need a tailored strategy. A professional can help you create a fly control protocol.

**Business Analogy**

Fly-like humans are those who are never still, but also never actually do anything useful. They're noisy and irritating, and they scrabble around in the muck and bring it into your home or office. They thrive on negativity, constantly complaining and spreading malicious gossip, while fixating on and amplifying problems without ever even trying to find solutions. Having one fly-like human in the office can seriously damage morale and productivity.

Much like the six-legged ones, managing two-legged flies is all about hygiene. Maintain a clean corporate culture, because if there's no "rot," there's nothing for them to feed on, and gossip dies when there's nothing toxic to spread. Also, as with the little airborne ones, the prevalence and behavior of human flies change as the environment changes. With real flies, it's seasonal and dependent on the time of day. This may or may not be the case with fly-like humans, but it's worth checking. Perhaps the particularly irritating behavior is most noticeable at the end of the month, the beginning of the day, or, for some reason you may not immediately be able to discern, worse on Wednesdays.

But the best way to control these irritating pests is to not let them into your office in the first place. You need a virtual air curtain, which means you need to carefully reconsider your management style and philosophy, rather than just doing what you've always done and hoping it continues to work. That's the business equivalent of leaving rotting meat in the yard for flies to breed in.

## Learning From Experience

Later in my career, soon after I started Pied Piper, I had a technician I'll call Jerry. On paper, Jerry wasn't the worst. He got his route done, turned in his workorders, and didn't rack up many callbacks. If you just looked at the numbers, he was average.

But Jerry had a different kind of impact—the buzzing kind. The moment he stepped into the office, the energy shifted. He'd flop down in the front office and start buzzing about every grievance he could think of—how messed up his schedule was, how he had too much drive time, and how the customers were impossible. He didn't just vent; he circled the room, pulling others into his orbit. Within minutes, two or three people were leaning on doorframes, nodding, laughing, and adding their own complaints. Hell, even out of the office, this guy would even buzz over his cell phone with other employees!

The problem wasn't that Jerry never had a real solution, even though he didn't. The problem was the noise. The constant complaining, the gossip, the negativity—it filled the air like a fly that just wouldn't land. Before long, I realized his buzzing was costing me more than a few minutes of chatter. Productivity dropped, morale sagged, and even customers started to notice slower response times.

One day, a newer tech came into my office and said, "I actually like the work, but I can't stand how negative it feels here. It's like everyone's waiting for Jerry to start complaining." That hit me hard. Jerry wasn't just irritating; he was contagious.

It doesn't take many flies to ruin a kitchen. One buzzing around can shut down a restaurant inspection, not because it eats the food, but because it contaminates the whole space. In the same way, Jerry wasn't ruining my business by himself, but he was contaminating the culture.

Eventually, I had to act. I pulled him in and laid it out straight: "You're costing this team more with your attitude and your amplified negative voice than you're helping with your route. That stops now, or we part ways." He didn't change, so eventually, we parted ways.

**The Lesson:** As a leader, you can't ignore the buzzers. They thrive on garbage, but only if you leave it lying around. If you let them in, they'll contaminate everything. Keep your house clean, and don't be afraid to swat when you have to.

## Quiet Underminers (Termites)

Termites are eusocial insects (which means they have a social structure that is complex) that eat cellulose and can silently destroy wooden structures from within. They play an essential role in nature by munching on dead trees so that they can decompose and help to create a vibrant and fertile soil environment. However, they're not quite so useful when they're munching away at the wooden frames of your house, your roof trusses, or the joists that hold up your floor. They can also eat furniture and picture frames. It's usually the stuff you don't move for a while. I had one client who was playing her grand piano when the leg collapsed because it had been eaten by termites. The worst part is that they're hidden, they're silent, and they're relentless. Unless you're lucky enough to see termites swarming to warn you of their presence, you'll only know about them when structural damage is present. Hopefully it won't be right after you've just bought that house you've been saving up for forever!

### Critter Control—Helpful Tips

In some parts of the US, popular wisdom is that there are two types of homes—those that have a termite problem and those that will. That's largely because most houses are made using primarily wood to frame their main structures, but even brick houses have wood framing, rafters, beams, and trusses. The best and only strategy is vigilance. Make it a habit to check for termites at least annually and more often if you live in a high-risk area with higher humidity and rain, you've had a termite problem before, or your house is old or aging. This is essential because, if you don't catch it early, the damage could be extensive and very expensive. And—here's a shocker—in the US, most household insurance will not cover termite damage.

You can try to do the inspection yourself if you know what to look for, but it's best to hire a professional. I've seen termite-infested wood and non-termite-infested wood in thousands of houses, so I, and most pest control professionals, can tell the difference with a great deal of confidence. It's not easy. I have to physically get into the crawl space and probe and sound the wood. Often, it looks fine from the outside, and it's only by tapping on it and probing it that you can tell it is not sound. And that discernment takes some practice. And, if you do have termites in your home or premises, termite treatment is not a good DIY project. Seriously, it's a big deal, so leave it to the pros.

## Business Analogy

One of the big problems with having termite-types in your organization is that you usually don't know about them until it's too late. These are the subversive employees who silently resist change—or promote unwanted change—often through subtle criticism or passive sabotage. They appear to be team players because, quite honestly, they are. They're just not on your team. They're quietly working together to undermine leadership or corporate culture, but staying well below the radar. Just like you need regular physical inspections to detect termites in your building structures, you need regular cultural inspections to detect these destructive employees. Make one-on-one performance reviews a regular thing, and set up feedback loops to reveal hidden threats. You have to do this because structural trust is such an essential part of business success; it's also what makes it hard to do this.

Trusting your employees and earning their trust is vital—trust works both ways. While checking up on them is necessary, remember to do so in a way that doesn't jeopardize their trust in you. In the same way that you don't tear down a home when you're sounding for termites, you can check up on employees in a way that does not imply you don't trust them. If regular reviews and feedback loops are a standard part of your day-to-day business practice, and they apply to everyone, no one needs to feel singled out. Make trust your default but, as the lovely Russian saying goes, "Trust, but verify."

Another reason to make checks routine is because you shouldn't make unsubstantiated assumptions. By that, I mean don't assume that your perfect employee who's been there forever is beyond reproach. The real insect parallel is the client who lives in a 100-year-old house, and says, "This house has been standing for a hundred years, and we've never had a termite problem. It's well-built, and my granddaddy used the best timbers." Sad to say, I've found termites in some of these gorgeous, well-built, old houses. Same inspection for everyone.

## Learning From Experience

When I was still climbing the corporate ladder, I worked with a supervisor I'll call Dan. He looked like a steady hand—always polite in meetings, never openly resistant, never one to stir up loud conflict. At first, I thought he was a model team player.

But over time, I started to notice something subtle. Projects that went through Dan's department always seemed to stall. His team missed deadlines more often, new initiatives lost steam when they landed on his desk, and employees who had been enthusiastic elsewhere suddenly became skeptical after working with him.

The tricky part was none of this was obvious. In fact, if you asked Dan directly, he'd tell you he fully supported every initiative. He'd nod in agreement during planning meetings and give all the right answers when upper management was watching. But behind the scenes, he was quietly eroding trust. He'd pull his team aside and say things like, "We'll give this a try, but don't worry—it'll probably blow over." Or "Just do the bare minimum. This isn't going to stick."

By the time I finally caught on, the damage had already been done. Morale in his department was shot. Deadlines slipped so often that other managers stopped depending on his team, which only fueled resentment. And I had to face the uncomfortable truth: Dan wasn't lazy or incompetent. He was quietly undermining the structure from within.

**The Lesson:** Termite-types don't make a lot of noise. They don't kick in doors or challenge leadership head-on. They just chew slowly and silently at the beams of trust, and by the time you notice, the damage can be extensive. What I learned is that regular cultural inspections are just as important as performance reviews. You don't wait for a roof to collapse before you check for termites, and you can't wait for a department to fail before you check for hidden underminers. Trust is essential, but trust without verification is just leaving your foundation unguarded.

## The Memory Eaters (Silverfish)

Silverfish are peculiar. It's such an attractive name; you have an image of a glorious trout leaping in the rapids, but they're actually small, wriggly, flightless insects that look a bit like miniature fish. And, yes, they are silver, but they're not pretty. They like hanging out in relatively moist environments, and they love eating paper and glue. They will happily munch away at files and documents, thereby destroying the memory of organizations. Because they like hanging out in moist places, they may only chew their way through your older files, such as archived ones. Well, you think, that's not that big a deal, but it is. Because the older files are probably the ones you haven't backed up electronically.

### Critter Control—Helpful Tips

Guard against these pests by keeping your archives neat and clean and checking any documents you bring into the office. Your best protection against these wiggly weirdos is a good dehumidifier, and your best insurance against the damage they can do is cloud storage—backed up by on-site and off-site physical digital storage.

### Business Analogy

Your clients, your accounts, your files, and your intellectual property are the basis of your business, but if you can't put your hand on a file, and easily and quickly extract the information in it, you may as well not have it. So the last things you want in a business are inept file clerks, sales reps who don't keep proper records, and project managers who spill coffee all over their paperwork. Or worse, all over their keyboards, and then find out they haven't done a backup for two weeks. You need to keep good records, safeguard customer information, and maintain an up-to-date and dynamic CRM (customer relations management) system. Without a good CRM system, your customers will miss services. Even worse, if they have a problem, but haven't heard from you in more than a year due to poor record keeping and a lack of proactive communication, they may take their business to a rival.

Guard what you know. Keep track of all paperwork by ensuring that reps, for example, sign for every order book, and that each and every page is accounted for. If a customer's file absolutely has to leave the office, make sure it is signed out and signed back in again.

It's also important to safeguard information even when it's not printed or documented digitally. Don't discuss employee issues with other employees, and don't talk about your clients with other clients. The best solution for information management is to store data digitally, but also to restrict access when necessary. Whenever possible, avoid the creation of sensitive information that can be easily passed from one person to another.

## Learning From Experience

Not having a good CRM was a big mistake I made early in my business. When I first started Pied Piper, we kept all our records on paper. Service tickets, customer notes, even follow-ups—they were all written out by hand and filed away. It wasn't that we weren't organized. In fact, we worked hard to stay on top of things, and for a while, it felt like the system was holding together.

But what I didn't realize was that memory is fragile when it lives only on paper. As our customer list grew, the files got fatter, the stacks of service slips got higher, and the filing cabinets started teetering ominously. Finding customer records took longer. We weren't forgetting people—we just weren't able to *see* everything clearly anymore. And in business, clarity is memory.

The turning point came when a longtime customer asked why she had to repeat the same issue every time she called in. She wasn't angry—yet—but I could tell she was frustrated. That conversation hit me like a gut punch. She was right. We had the information, but it was buried in stacks of tickets and files. To her, it looked like we weren't paying attention.

That's when it clicked: I should have gone automated from the very beginning. I thought CRM systems were for the big players, the companies with thousands of accounts. I told myself, *We're still small, we can get by.* But what I didn't realize was that one customer is the beginning of your memory, and if you don't build the right habits early, catching up later is painful.

When we finally made the move to automation, the difference was night and day. Suddenly, every customer's history was at our fingertips—every note, every service, every promise.

But getting there wasn't easy. We had to backfill years of handwritten records, scan, sort, and upload mountains of paper. It felt like digging through boxes the silverfish had already chewed through—slow, tedious, and costly.

I learned that the silverfish I should have been guarding against was my own complacency. Yes, like I said earlier, don't forget to look in the mirror because sometimes you, as the manager, may be the problem.

**The Lesson:** Silverfish don't destroy new paper; they eat away at the older files you assume are safe. In business, the same is true of memory. I learned that the best time to invest in a CRM system is not when you're "big enough," but when you get your first customer. Because every note matters, and if you don't protect your history from the beginning, you'll spend years trying to rebuild what you should have preserved all along.

## The Flock Followers (Pigeons And Starlings)

Pigeons and starlings are highly social, adaptable birds that can virtually take over buildings and precincts as well as parts of some cities, like a scene from Alfred Hitchcock's horror movie *The Birds,* with their noise, constant movement, and sheer weight of numbers. Many people love pigeons, and tourists often feed them in city squares. But, of course, what pigeons eat, they have to excrete, and they do that with great enthusiasm. Starlings are similar, but not as much loved. They are invasive and disruptive to ecosystems.

One bird is not usually a problem; it's when they gather en masse, and of course, the worst part about lots of birds in one place is lots of bird poop in one place. It's unsightly, it can be a slip hazard in wet weather, and it can damage property and infrastructure. Bird poop is acidic, so it can eat through the paint on cars, and it can build up to a significant thickness if not dealt with. And, no, contrary to folklore, I don't believe it's good luck if it lands on you. Along with nesting materials, it can clog gutters and downpipes, which can cause catastrophic leaks. The accumulation of bird nesting materials can also increase the risk of fires and the chances of bird mites entering buildings.

Birds can also transmit disease. They can carry bird flu, although you'd have to spend a lot of time cooped up in a small space with them to catch it. Of more concern, though, is histoplasmosis. This fungus lives happily in bird poop and becomes airborne whenever the poop is disturbed, for example, when it's cleaned off surfaces.

While all the above is true for both starlings and pigeons, starlings can be particularly irritating, especially in domestic environments. They're sociable and gregarious, so they like to nest close to each other, taking over a whole tree or even two or three neighboring trees, downtown plazas, and shopping centers. And then, they gossip incessantly all night. If you have these guys in your garden, you're not likely to get any sleep at all. And if you have them outside your business premises, they may well run off guests and customers.

**Critter Control—Helpful Tips**

One or two birds is no big deal, but dealing with a large flock or a long-term infestation is best left up to the experts. Any area that is significantly contaminated with bird poop must be cleaned very carefully. I won't go near a deposit of bird poop without considering what type of personal protective equipment (PPE) is required, and neither will any other pest control professional. So I strongly suggest you don't just go in and scrape off the accumulated bird poo on your building. Histoplasmosis is relatively rare and usually mild, but it can be very serious, causing pneumonia-like symptoms and even death.

As with most pests, prevention is the best strategy. If you see one bird roosting close by, keep an eye open for more. If one turns to three, and the next day there are five, you should start considering ways to discourage them from nesting on your property.

Bird netting on overhangs, windows, and other openings keeps them from entering warehouses and other buildings. Repellents and spikes make ledges unattractive places for them to hang out. If you think spikes are a bit—well—visually aggressive, bird slopes work by changing the angle of a ledge so the birds can't roost comfortably there, and they don't make your premises look like the county jail. For a flock that isn't getting the message, it might be time to take off the kid gloves and put up jolt tracks that give them a mild (nonlethal) electric shock. You can also install a sound system that broadcasts bird distress calls, or predator calls, both of which usually have the feathered fiends beating a hasty retreat and flying off somewhere else. You could also consider installing rotating reflective bird repellers on your roof. Reflective tape on windows has also been shown to deter birds from landing on window ledges.

## Business Analogy

In any business, you want your staff to buy into the company culture and to get along with each other, but you also want them to be creative individuals who bring their own contribution to the whole. Such employees create value through diversity, creativity, and independence of thought.

What you don't want is a bunch of bird-brained flutterers who, like pigeons, mindlessly follow the crowd or a bunch of invasive starling-types disrupting harmony by displacing useful people.

Pigeon-people turn your meetings into a gaggling lovefest of groupthink where noise displaces value and creative thought. Mindless peer pressure creates inward-looking teams with biases and prejudices that limit creativity, and your office becomes noisy, messy, and social. Not every "team player" builds teams. Some just like the noise.

Protect your company from these noisy, non-contributing "team players" by creating a culture that values contribution over social dominance and popularity. It's not going to be easy, and you may need to employ a metaphorical scarecrow, in the form of a meeting chair who can clip the wings of noisy non-contributors, or pretty shiny rotating bling-bling bird repellents in the form of performance reviews that accurately reflect real contribution rather than noise.

**Learning From Experience**

One of my earliest shocks at Pied Piper was how much customers could act like a flock of pigeons. I thought each account would stand on its own, but I quickly learned that in many markets, especially tight-knit communities, customers move together.

There was one neighborhood in particular where this lesson hit me hard. I had landed my first big residential account—a customer who loved our service and was quick to recommend us. Soon after, I picked up a few more houses on the same street. And then a few more. Things were looking good.

Then, one spring, a competitor came through knocking on doors with an aggressive price promotion. It didn't take long before the phone started ringing. Not one call, but three, then five. Almost the entire block wanted to cancel or "pause" service to switch to the cheaper deal. It was like watching pigeons take flight—all at once, all in the same direction.

The sting wasn't just the cancellations; it was the realization that we hadn't built strong enough ties with each household individually. They weren't thinking as loyal customers of Pied Piper; they were thinking as part of a flock that moved wherever the first bird landed.

That experience taught me two things. First, you can't rely solely on referrals and group momentum, because that same momentum can turn against you. Second, you have to invest in every single customer relationship as if they're your only one. If each homeowner had felt a direct connection—through consistent follow-ups, clear value, and personalized care—the competitor's promotion wouldn't have been enough to spook them.

**The Lesson:** Pigeons and starlings aren't dangerous one at a time; it's when they gather that they overwhelm buildings, sidewalks, and even whole city blocks. Customers can do the same. A flock of accounts gained quickly can be lost just as quickly if you don't anchor each relationship individually. In business, don't just win the flock. Win the bird. Because, if you don't, they'll all take off together when any one of them is spooked for any reason at all. And cleaning up after them, or rustling them back into the coop, is always harder than keeping them grounded in the first place.

## The Hustlers (Ants)

So small, but so irritating. It's amazing how ants can just take over a space. Like many pests, you may not realize the full extent of your problem until it gets completely out of hand. The ones you see busily hustling to and from the break room carrying sugar grains or bread crumbs twice their weight are just the surface. Follow the trail, and see where they take all that stuff and you may find multiple colonies, often in the most surprising places. Ants don't like to get too cold, so if they have a choice, they'll build their nests somewhere warm— like behind your server. Or *in* your server. That's right, all the electrical and electronic equipment in your office emits heat, which creates a nanoclimate that's just perfect for ants. And you won't know about it until your system shuts down or goes haywire.

There are lots of terrible things you can say about ants, but you can't say they're lazy. These guys are constantly on the move, hustling backwards and forwards along neatly defined routes, rubbing antennae together whenever they meet up, and then continuing on their mysterious missions. Always busy. Busy, busy, busy.

## Critter Control—Helpful Tips

There are many different kinds of ants, and how you deal with them depends largely on which particular ant you have as an unwanted guest. The ones you are most likely to come across in the US are carpenter ants, little black ants, odorous house ants (the name says it all), pavement ants, pharaoh ants, fire ants, and thief ants.

Little black ants are native to the US, so they usually live outside, but they can invade homes if life gets too hard out in the wild. Carpenter ants use tiny bits of wood to make their nests, so they quietly take apart your residence to make it their own. Over time, they can be very destructive, and before you know it, your house may be falling down around your ears. Odorous house ants just loooove sugar. Most ants do, of course, but these guys are the real junk food junkies. And they're well-named, so don't crush them because they stink and your house will smell like rotten coconuts. Pavement ants are not usually a problem indoors, because they live in and under paving, but they can be if they get into the walls. Fire ants are rarely found in houses, but you might be unlucky enough to have them in your yard. These are the guys that really spoil picnics and my son's football practice when he was 11—ouch! All the other ants just steal the devilled eggs, but fire ants actually attack you, adding injury to insult. And they are also well-named. Their bites really sting and leave a nasty itchy spot that lasts for days. Pharoah ants, which get their name because they were (probably mistakenly) believed to be one of the biblical plagues of ancient Egypt, are often found in homes because they love starchy, sugary foods. Thief ants are the Atkins/Banting disciples of the ant world, because unlike all the rest, they are not wild about sugary foods. Instead, they prefer high-fat, high-protein foods; they really enjoy empty pizza boxes with all that delicious cheese and oil stuck to the lid (but they certainly wouldn't turn up their nonexistent noses at a full pizza box).

Not as common—yet—are Raspberry crazy ants. These recent invaders, which were first found near Houston in 2002, are rapidly spreading across the southern part of the US, displacing native insects, smothering baby animals, ruining farmland and pastures, and destroying infrastructure, especially electronics. I am just one of the local pest control professionals in Texas who are trying to control the spread of these nasty little bugs. It would be great if we could eliminate them completely, but I think that will be difficult.

Ants are mostly a problem in kitchens, or where there's food, but they can fool you. I was once called to an immaculately clean and tidy house in San Antonio where the bedroom closet was infested with pharoah ants. Interestingly, it was only on the husband's side, because the greedy little critters were attracted to the heavy starch that was added by the dry cleaning service to his jeans and shirts.

If you can accurately identify the invader, you might be able to tackle a low to mild ant infestation yourself by simply buying and applying the right product from a reputable supplier. But be aware: You can have more than one kind of ant in the house; however, they will usually be in different rooms, or at least different places.

If you're not sure about identifying them, or there are just too many, it's best to call in the pros. We deal with this stuff every day.

As with most little intruders, prevention is the best strategy. Don't leave delicious food scraps lying around, bearing in mind that unwashed dishes are veritable treasure troves of delicious food scraps. Tackle any infestation as soon as it rears its pesky, antenna-wiggling head, and constantly keep a look out for ants in your yard and against the foundation walls of your house. Check under sinks, long baseboards, and window seals, and in the garage. Move electronic equipment every couple of months just to check that a colony of ants hasn't made itself comfortable in the nice, safe, warm, sheltered space hidden underneath it.

## Business Analogy

In the business environment, you're not really concerned about colonies of ant-people; it's more about people who are always busy but never seem to achieve anything. Their desk is neat and tidy and they spend ages color-coordinating their files, but it's a system only they can understand and, even then, they're not so sure about it. They can also take two days to send an email because they are constantly editing and reediting it until it's perfect. And already out of date. And when that happens, they'll console themselves by creating a new color-coordinated system for storing stationery items in their desks.

Or it's the off-site tech who spends hours polishing their truck, cleaning their equipment, and doing extensive surveys, so it's ages before any actual work gets done. Or the rep who calls a second and a third lead before they've closed the first, and then forgetting to follow up the first, and calling a fourth lead because it seems so promising, and—hey—number five on the list looks like a good prospect. Lots of leads, lots of calls, lots of proposals, loads of work, but no orders or sales

So, yeah, these people are definitely not lazy; they're just disorganized, unfocused, and undisciplined. If you can successfully set up systems to harness and direct all that energy, you'll have a winner, so it's worth working on these ant-people. Set up structures, well-defined key performance indicators, and accountability, so that all work is focused, followed up, and productive.

**Learning From Experience**

Soon after starting Pied Piper, I learned that not all "busy" customers are good customers. Some are what I call ant-customers—always moving, always asking, always hustling you for more, but never actually committing.

There was one property manager in particular—let's call him Anton. He called me constantly. Every week, there was another request: "Can you give me a quote for this building?", "Can you come inspect the warehouse?", and "What would it cost if we added rodent stations over here?" Each request sounded promising. Each time, I thought, *This is going to turn into a big account.*

But the problem was, it never did. He'd gather my proposals, ask for follow-ups, and then disappear. A month later, he'd resurface with another "urgent" request. I finally realized he wasn't building a relationship—he was building a pile of information, maybe to shop around, maybe just to keep himself busy. Either way, it was hustle without outcome.

The cost to me was real. Every trip, every quote, every inspection was time and energy we could have spent with paying customers who actually valued our service. Just like ants carrying crumbs back and forth across the counter, all that busyness didn't amount to anything nourishing. It was motion, not progress.

Eventually, I had to draw a line. I told Anton, "I'd be glad to work with you, but before I keep running out proposals, we need a decision on what you want us to do." That was the turning point. He either had to commit or move on. He never did become a customer, but the lesson stuck with me.

Hustle without results is just wasted energy. Ants can overwhelm you with activity, but unless that activity is carrying value back to the colony, it's meaningless. In business, not every potential customer deserves unlimited hustle. Sometimes the best service you can give is clarity. Set boundaries, focus on those who commit, and don't let the busy ants distract you from the real work of building lasting relationships.

## The Master Manipulators (Spiders)

So many people are totally freaked out by spiders, there's even a word for it—arachnaphobia, fear of spiders. There's something about the way they move, their hairy legs, and their silent, sinister strategy of lying in wait for unsuspecting victims. But they are also remarkable creatures that play an important role in maintaining biodiversity, mostly by preying on insects and other pests, thereby preventing overpopulation. They also pollinate some plants.

But they are undeniably eerie. They're (mostly) solitary, and they're (mostly) silent ambush hunters that carefully and patiently build elaborate webs to ensnare unwary prey. And once they've caught their unwilling lunch, they'll slowly devour it, sometimes while it's still alive. That's not quite as bad as it sounds, because spider venom acts as an anesthetic. Or at least a paralytic, which isn't quite so nice because it just means the prey can't move. I'm not doing a good job of talking spiders up, am I? But, seriously, in the wild, they are a good thing. Also, many cultures consider spiders to be beneficial and consider killing one to be bad luck. The Native American dream catcher, for example, is a stylized spider web that is traditionally hung over a child's crib to catch bad dreams and bad spirits, thus protecting the child.

Spiders also play a practical protective role. They eat nasty insects like flies and malaria-carrying mosquitoes, and they rarely bite humans. Interestingly, some industries welcome spiders. Wine cellars and distillers, for example, welcome spiders because their webs entrap any wood-boring beetles as they fly in but before they can lay eggs in the barrels and start a whole dynasty of alcoholic-boring beetles. And you thought those stylish spider webs in traditional wine cellars were just for show to make the place look old. It's probably an exaggeration, but some wine estates proudly claim that their cobwebs date back to the 17th century.

But, even if they do keep down flies and their webs add to the ambience of ancient tradition in trendy-trad wine cellars, they do not look good in a city apartment or a suburban home.

## Critter Control—Helpful Tips

Keeping spiders out of your house is all about simple hygiene and good housekeeping. Keeping spaces clean and uncluttered will make your home uninviting to spiders. Most spiders are solitary, so you're not likely to find more than one or two in your house at any one time. I deal with spiders often as a pest control professional; however, most people can handle getting rid of one or two spiders themselves. And if not, it's a good opportunity to make friends with your more rugged neighbors.

The best way to get rid of a spider is with the tried-and-tested jar-and-cardboard technique. Sneak up on the spider, put a wide-mouthed glass jar over it, slide a piece of cardboard under the jar to trap the spider, then take it outside and release it far from the house. If you have unsightly webs, you can get rid of them with a broom, feather duster, or a vacuum cleaner. If you have an infestation of lots of spiders, contact a pest control specialist, or consider selling the movie rights, because that is a whole new level of strange.

## Business Analogy

Spiders get a bad rap in traditional storytelling. There's the probably not malicious one that frightened Miss Muffet and—much more sinisterly—the one who sweetly and innocently says to the unsuspecting fly, "Will you walk into my parlour?" And we all know how that's going to end for the fly. Probably the most interesting and most pertinent spider for my argument is Anansi, a mischievous, trickster-like mythical character who subverts cultural norms, causes havoc, and outsmarts more powerful people by using wit, charm, and cunning. Originally from West Africa, Anansi was transported to the US aboard slave ships and still has a place in African American traditions.

And these are the spider-people you may find in your organizations. Like Anansi, they plot and then lie in wait for unwary colleagues to fall for their tricks. Like the fly-inviting spider, they spend days, weeks, even months, building webs of intrigue and influence before sweetly inviting their prey within. These are the people who spin webs of lies, misinformation, and suspicion about colleagues and put traps in the way of unwary subordinates or even bosses. They gain success by ruthlessly climbing the corporate ladder by strategically ensnaring all competitors, or quietly, subtly, and skillfully poaching clients from other sales reps. They sabotage other people's projects by offering support but then withholding it. They break promises. They are charming and predatory, charismatic manipulators who use charm or information as leverage, constantly plotting, pulling strings, and trapping others in obligation or confusion. These strategic lone wolves play office politics instead of actively and effectively pursuing shared goals.

Getting rid of these spider-characters is difficult, because like Anansi, they are charming and disarming. Just like keeping real spiders out of your home requires cleanliness, hygiene and regular decluttering, preventing spider-people from destroying your business requires good policies, an unambiguous corporate structure, clear communication, and well-defined processes.

Don't allow yourself to be derailed by charm; always opt for character over charisma, substance over style, and steak over sizzle. Remove the metaphorical webs that obscure standard procedures, and build real value with your clients and your team.

In the same way that some cultures consider spiders to be good luck and happily cohabit with them because they kill much nastier critters like malaria-carrying mosquitoes, it may be worth keeping your spider-pest, but only if you can harness that shrewd cunningness to the advantage of your team. Perhaps, like Spider-Man's uncle Ben explained to the young Peter Parker, you should remind your spider-pests that "With great power comes great responsibility." After all, even the uber mischievous Anansi is renowned for using his subversive cunning to ultimately do good.

## Learning From Experience

Soon after starting Pied Piper, I learned that not every vendor was a partner. Some are what I call spider vendors—masters at spinning webs of promises, charm, and half-truths until you're tangled in commitments you never meant to make.

There was one rep in particular who stands out. I'll call him Peter. He promised his product would save me money, outperform anything else on the market, and come with all kinds of "extras"—training, support, even marketing help. He made it sound like saying yes was the obvious choice. And at first, I believed him. Every conversation felt smooth, every offer sweetened just enough to pull me in further.

But over time, the cracks showed. The product wasn't saving us money. The extras came with strings attached. And when I pressed for accountability, he suddenly wasn't as quick to return calls. I realized I hadn't built a partnership—I had stepped into a web. He hadn't won with value; he had won with patience, weaving threads until I was too entangled to notice.

The cost was real. My team wasted time adjusting to a system that didn't deliver, and we lost opportunities chasing promises that never came true. That was the moment I made a change. Since then, I've vetted all vendors the same way I do prospective employees. They are measured, held accountable, and have to prove their worth over time. Charm doesn't count. Results do. Focus on business, not friendship, when dealing with vendors.

**The Lesson:** Spiders don't destroy with force—they trap with soft, subtle, but strong webs. In business, manipulative vendors do the same. They use charm and promises to catch you, and by the time you see the truth, you're already stuck. The only way to avoid the web is to set clear standards from the start: Demand proof, measure results, and never confuse charm and value.

While spider bites are rarely fatal, they hurt a lot and can make you very sick, but they rarely bite humans. But there are some critters that, while they also don't often actually intentionally attack humans, can cause pain, harm, and even death. These are the assailants, assassins, and insurgents attacking at the heart of organizations—usually at the people in them.

# CHAPTER 4

# Assailants—Predators Attacking at the Heart of Organizations

Assailants are genuinely dangerous animals that can cause serious harm, pain, or even death to humans. That sounds pretty daunting, but most of these truly heavyweight threats don't attack unless provoked, so you shouldn't lose too much sleep thinking about them. Honestly, except for bees, most people go their whole lives without ever coming into contact with any of these scary creatures.

## Triggered Defenders (Bees)

Bees are incredibly useful, wonderful creatures, and they are essential to our continued survival on this planet. They pollinate about one-third of the plants we depend on for food, so without them, we would starve. And, as a bonus, they produce honey. What's not to love? Okay, granted, they can sting, but bees only sting when they believe they are under attack. It really is a last resort because they can only sting once, and stinging causes their death. Sure, a bee sting hurts, but it hurts the bee more.

## Critter Control—Helpful Tips

Bees are wonderful, and many people live with wild hives in their yards, taking it as a compliment to their gardening skills. So if you have bees nesting close to your home, consider leaving them. But, if they have infiltrated the structure of your house or you are allergic to bee stings, you may want to remove them. The best way is to contact a local beekeeper who may relocate the entire hive, but, if you have no luck there, contact a pest control professional. My company has moved quite a few beehives, but we have a secret weapon. One of our employees is a master beekeeper, so we involve him in all bee-related calls, and he gladly takes over the hives when possible.

Reputable pest control companies shouldn't use lethal means as the first option to control bees unless they pose an immediate threat to the public and there is absolutely no other alternative. But that would also depend on where you're located, because different states have different regulations about bee removal and disposal. The bottom line is that bees are not pests, they are beneficial contributors that deserve our gratitude and protection.

## Business Analogy

If you have a honey bee, or a small swarm of honey bees in your office, be thankful. They work tirelessly, have great team spirit, produce sweet results, and sting only when provoked. However, you should keep a careful eye out for robber bees.

These are sneaky rogue bees that hijack the fruits of all your hard work. Within the company, a robber bee might be a salesperson who poaches other people's leads or a team member who cunningly manages to claim the credit for work they haven't done. Perhaps even more dangerous, though, are the robber bees from competing companies.

Just like the real robber bees, these people are opportunists and keep a careful eye out for a hive that's been weakened. These human sneaks notice when you or your team loses focus. When times are lean and things are getting bad, that's when they swoop in and steal your clients from under your nose. Or they'll offer to help after you've done almost all the work by putting in the final touches and then claiming credit for the whole project. Protect yourself from these pests by only accepting help if you really need it, and then do so on your own terms. Don't let robber bee-people steal all your honey.

Unlike real bees, human robbers are unlikely to actually kill you, but also unlike real bees, some of them are naturally aggressive and actually do enjoy inflicting pain. And, also like bees, they are at their most dangerous when they gang up on you.

Another reason robber bees are such a problem is that, unlike a responsible beekeeper who will ensure they leave enough honey for the hive, robbers take and take with no sense of proportion. As a business owner, you need to make sure that you are paying your employee-bees well, and that the sales-bees get a decent commission. In other words, make sure they have enough "honey" to survive because it is when times are tough and there's not enough sweetness to go round that bees go rogue and become robbers. Some beekeepers who take too much honey act surprised when the colony collapses and dies, and blame the bees for not making enough honey. It's the same in business. If you don't pay your employees what they're worth, they'll vote with their feet and find a metaphorical hive with more metaphorical honey.

Bees really are a lesson in compassionate HR. Think about the loyal warrior bee who stings to defend the hive, knowing it will cost her her life. This may be pushing the analogy a bit here, but loyal humans who are pushed too much may contribute so much to the hive that they run the risk of burnout and can seriously compromise their health. Loyalty should be recognized and rewarded.

## Learning From Experience

When I was a branch manager in the corporate world, I had a technician I'll call Sam. He was one of the most loyal employees I have ever managed. Sam showed up early, stayed late, and never said no when someone needed help. If a customer called at the last minute, he'd volunteer. If another tech fell behind, he'd jump in to cover their stops. On the surface, Sam was the perfect honeybee—always busy, always producing, always protecting the hive.

But like real bees, Sam had a trigger. He didn't complain, but the pressure built quietly. The endless overtime, the skipped lunches, the constant "just one more stop." Eventually, one small misunderstanding with the front office set him off. He exploded. He slammed his clipboard down and threatened to quit on the spot. To anyone watching, it looked like an overreaction. But to me, it was a warning. I had pushed a loyal defender past his breaking point.

The problem wasn't Sam. The problem was me. I had mistaken loyalty for unlimited capacity, and when you do that, even the best honeybees can turn into triggered defenders. They sting, and that sting hurts everyone—the employee, the team, and the business.

I had to change how I managed the team. We restructured schedules, made sure overtime was shared more evenly, and encouraged time off before burnout hit. Sam stayed with us, and he became one of my most reliable people. But that moment stuck with me. It reminded me that loyalty doesn't mean limitless, and pushing too hard can destroy the very people you depend on most.

**The Lesson**: Bees are some of the most valuable creatures on the planet, but even they sting when provoked. In business, loyal employees are the same. They'll work hard, defend the team, and give everything they have—sometimes more than they should. But if you push too hard, ignore the signs, or take their loyalty for granted, the sting will come. As leaders, our job isn't just to collect honey; it's to protect the hive and care for the bees who make it thrive.

## Yellow Jackets and Other Wasps

Yellow jackets, like bees, play an important ecological role. Even though they can't produce honey and may not be nearly as well-loved as bees, yellow jackets have value and should be treated well, rewarded, and not intentionally provoked.

However, they do have nasty stings, so they need to be carefully handled, especially as they can sting more than once.

## Critter Control—Helpful Tips

Unlike the sweet honey bee that only stings in extremis, yellow jackets and other wasps can safely sting first and ask questions later. Thankfully, they usually mind their own business as long as they're not provoked or harassed—a lesson I had to learn the hard way. I once had a colony of yellow jackets in my lawn and didn't realize it until I'd pushed the lawnmower over the nest entrance. And then, boy, did I notice! I had about 30 painful welts on my legs and—wow—they hurt. But after a few days, the pain subsided and I was none the worse, which is more than I can say for the yellow jackets. I confess, I went all Rambo on them.

All wasps, including yellow jackets, are best dealt with at night, when they are less active and less reactive. So, once the sun had set, with my legs still burning, I went out onto the lawn to pinpoint the entrance to the nest. Then I exacted some chemical revenge, choosing the full drench method. That was not only because I had vengeance in my heart, but also because it's almost impossible to tell how deep the nest is, so it's better to be safe than sorry. If you've ever wondered where the term "overkill" originated, now you know.

Removing a wasp nest is not that tricky if it's a small one, so your best strategy is constant surveillance to catch them when they just start building. If you have a regular inspection for other critters, your pest control professional will do that as part of the process and will inform you if they find something.

## Business Analogy

Like I said, yellow jackets and other wasps are no problem as long as you let them carry on with their lives and don't step on their proverbial toes. And it's the same with quick-to-anger but otherwise easygoing employees.

I like to work in a disciplined but relaxed work environment where everyone feels safe and valued. I chat with every new employee after they've been with us for about a week, just to check in. One of the questions I always ask is, "What makes you angry?" And then I pay attention to the answer to ensure that neither I nor any other employee pokes that sensitive spot. I think this is common sense, but you'd be surprised how uncommon it is. I've met managers who constantly press their employees' buttons, just to "keep them on their toes." They like an environment of hostility and competitiveness, especially in commission-based roles, because it keeps their employees hungry. And, they believe, hungry employees bring in more business. I disagree.

I think hungry employees are angry employees, and I don't think anger is productive.

## Learning From Experience

At Pied Piper, I make it a point to learn what triggers my people. Everyone has something that sets them off—an invisible line that, if crossed, turns a good day into a bad one. And as a leader, if you don't know where that line is, you'll eventually cross it by accident.

I work with a technician I'll call Jack, who is a solid performer. The customers love him, his production is steady, and he takes pride in his work. But I learned quickly that nothing makes Jack angrier than feeling like his time is wasted. If his schedule isn't organized or if he gets bounced around with last-minute changes, it eats at him.

One morning, dispatch accidentally sent him across town twice in the same day for jobs that could've been grouped together. To Jack, it looked like no one cared about the extra miles or the strain it put on him. By the time he got back to the office, he was fired up. He didn't hold back either. He let everyone know exactly how he felt.

It would've been easy to write it off as an overreaction. But the truth is, he had told me that disorganized scheduling was one of his biggest frustrations at his previous employer. We didn't listen, and it cost us: Clients were lost as a result.

That was a reminder: If you don't pay attention to your employees' triggers, you'll get stung. Since then, we've tightened scheduling and given techs more input on their routes. Jack cooled off, and he's still one of my most reliable people. But I won't forget that lesson.

**The Lesson:** Yellow jackets and other wasps sting when you disturb their nest. Employees do too. Knowing what makes your people mad isn't optional; it's leadership. It's how you prevent blowups, build trust, and keep good employees from walking out the door. If you ignore those triggers, don't be surprised when the sting comes.

# The Prickly Loners (Scorpions)

Scorpions are the archetypal loners. They live in the wild places where the sun bakes the land in the day and the nights are frigid. Antisocial by nature, if they feel crowded or frightened, they let you know by bringing up their tail in a threatening gesture. That's one thing about scorpions: They're honest. They even let you know how lethal they are, since —generally—their level of venomousness is relative to the thickness of their tails. Seems obvious, if you think about it: The ones with skinny little pincers and fat tails are more likely to be venomous than the ones with skinny tails and huge, powerful pincers. It's true on average, but don't depend on that, and even the less venomous ones can inflict an agonizing sting.

They are fearsome predators that live mostly on bugs and other invertebrates, but they can bring down something as big as a mouse. (I couldn't resist that. How often do you get to say "as big as a mouse," and mean big?) A sting from even the most venomous scorpion is not likely to kill a healthy adult, but it will make them regret doing whatever brought them into contact with the stinger.

## Critter Control—Helpful Tips

Scorpions will sometimes wander into houses in the fall as evening temperatures drop, especially in the warmer states. It's not an everyday occurrence, but it does happen—particularly in brick or stone homes, since those walls hold and radiate heat just like the rocks the scorpions would hide under in the wild. If they hadn't gone soft and become house scorpions, that is.

Therefore, if you do come across a scorpion, it's more likely to be when you're working in the yard, out camping, or hiking. So take some commonsense precautions when out in the wild. When collecting firewood, for example, always turn over dead logs with a stick before picking them up, and never pick up a piece of dead wood by sliding your hand under it. That's just asking for trouble. It's also a good idea to look carefully under your tent or tarp before packing it away in the morning and shake out your shoes before putting them on. Basically, carefully check any sheltered spot a scorpion could be hiding.

## Business Analogy

Scorpion employees are those invisible, quiet people that you hardly ever notice, but they often tend to be critical to the successful operation of your business. They're the IT specialists who work in some back room like a scorpion living under a rock in the desert. They're the janitors who know everyone's secrets because they see everything, but are almost never seen themselves. They're the file clerk who quietly does what they're asked day in, day out, never questioning, never commenting. And everything goes fine until, one day, someone corners them or stands on them. Then the mild-mannered clerk could turn whistleblower, the janitor could tell the HR manager's spouse what they find in their office every Thursday morning, and the IT tech could cause untold havoc if they were to raise their tail and strike.

As a manager, remember that being solitary is fine, especially in some fields, like IT, but it's not a good idea to forget about people. So check in regularly. Daily, weekly, monthly, whatever works well for your scorpion. With the technology available, there's no excuse, but try to check in physically, too, as often as you can. I find a handshake gives me the warmth and strength of a person, a look in the eye gives me a view into their soul and their feelings, and their voice tells me how things are going in their lives. Don't ask "How're you doing?" if you don't want the answer, and don't say "Call me if you need anything," if you don't mean it.

Always pay attention to the keeper of the keys, the guardian of the secrets, and the washer of the dirty linen. This is how you prevent the rise of the invisible meek and the revenge of the nerds.

## Learning From Experience

I've learned that not every employee wants to be front and center. Some prefer the shadows, working quietly in their own space, handling the jobs nobody else sees but everybody depends on. They're solitary, low-profile, but absolutely essential.

I think of one in particular; I'll call her Dana. Dana wasn't the loudest in meetings. She didn't spend time in the breakroom swapping stories. She came in, did her job, and slipped out at the end of the day. At first glance, you might have thought she was disengaged, but the truth was, she kept critical pieces of our operation running smoothly. She was the one double-checking paperwork before it went out and catching errors that could have cost us big with regulators. She was the one making sure licenses were filed on time, insurance documents were renewed, and safety audits didn't fall through the cracks.

Most people didn't notice her, until one day a manager snapped at her over a scheduling mistake that wasn't hers. I'll never forget the look when her "tail came up." She didn't yell or storm out, but her sting was sharp. She quietly laid out every detail of what she'd been managing behind the scenes, how many mistakes she had prevented from becoming disasters, and how little recognition she had received in return. For a moment, the entire room went silent. The sting had landed.

That moment hit me hard. It reminded me that quiet doesn't mean unimportant and solitary doesn't mean disengaged. It means leaders have to look under the rocks. We have to check in on the people who keep things running in the background, even if they never ask for attention. Because if you ignore them—or worse, upset them—you'll feel the sting.

**The Lesson:** Scorpions don't attack without cause, but when provoked, they strike with precision and pain. In business, your quiet employees are the same. They carry secrets, responsibilities, and unseen burdens. If you value them, support them, and check in regularly, they'll remain your strongest hidden allies. But if you step on them carelessly, the sting will remind you just how powerful they really are.

## The Big Squeeze (Pythons)

It's estimated that there are more Burmese pythons in Florida than there are in what was Burma, but is now called Myanmar. In Asia, the snakes do well because they're part of a complex ecosystem that evolved alongside them. But when they first set their slithery selves into the Florida Everglades, they landed in python heaven: a hot, steamy climate with miles and miles of wetlands, and no natural predators. Christmas! They flourished, preying on white-tailed deer, raccoons, birds, house cats, rabbits, pet dogs, and even small alligators. They're constrictors that crush their prey; so while they are unlikely to eat humans, they can do some serious damage and could even kill a person. It's best to keep your distance.

## Critter Control—Helpful Tips

I deal with snakes in my business from time to time, but this is not my field of expertise, and most pest control companies wouldn't even return your phone call for a snake callout. I strongly suggest you try to identify the species if you find one in your home because you may want to let them be. If you can take a good photo of it, you can even identify it online. Many snakes are not venomous, and they serve as a useful biological control by eating rats and other small rodents. But don't assume anything with snakes. Always get an expert to identify any snake on your property and do a risk-benefit analysis.

The Burmese pythons are another story. They do not belong in Florida, and because they pose a major threat to indigenous wildlife, there is a reward for capturing them. There's even an official ten-day Florida Python Challenge with fabulous prizes. But don't think you're going to head down to the Everglades, knock back a few beers, and catch yourself a python because these guys are biiiiiig. Also, don't be tempted to get one as a pet or a dance partner. The former is silly, and the latter stupid. These snakes are huge, powerful predators with a short temper. They are not venomous, but they can and do bite, but that's not the real threat. They are almost pure muscle, and they use that muscle to crush their prey, so they can easily crush a human, even a large adult. The general rule of thumb for dealing with live constrictors is one strong man per meter of snake, and Burmese pythons can grow to six or seven meters (up to 20 or so feet).

## Business Analogy

The human python equivalent are the dull, faceless corporations that destroy small businesses and are particularly threatening to local, family-owned service businesses like yours. As a small business, you can't hope to fight these behemoths on your own. Like I said, it can take six or seven strong men to wrestle a full-grown python. If you're going to tackle big corporations, you should connect with other small businesses, your local chamber of commerce or trade association, industry-specific alliances, faith groups, and other local civic groups. If you don't, these large corporations will eliminate the small family businesses that are so much a part of small-town communities the same way Burmese pythons are destroying the sensitive Everglades ecosystem. Don't let that happen.

Also, be aware of so-called "angel investors" who use their economic influence to destroy or damage small businesses by giving advice that is not in the best interests of the small business owner or entrepreneur. If given the chance, these unwelcome intruders will squeeze the life out of family businesses and ruin the economic landscape of small towns.

## Learning From Experience

Fortunately, I have not been squeezed out by bigger companies, but I have seen it happen to other businesses. What I have learned, though, is that the squeeze doesn't always come from competitors. Sometimes it often comes from the pressures we put on ourselves.

I remember a season at Pied Piper when we tried to do it all at once. We were adding new services, expanding into fresh markets, upgrading vehicles, and saying yes to every opportunity that came our way. At first, it didn't feel like much. One new service here, an equipment upgrade there, another project that looked too good to pass up. Each one by itself seemed manageable. On paper, it looked like growth but, slowly, the pressure built. It felt like we were getting squeezed tighter every day. Cash flow was stretched, and even simple decisions started to feel heavy. That's the thing about a python: It doesn't kill you with one big strike. It squeezes a little at a time, until your ribs crack, and you realize you can't breathe.

One day it hit me. We weren't building smarter; we were just piling more weight on ourselves. I could feel the focus slipping, the energy draining, and the pressure becoming too much. That's when I knew we had to change.

We hit pause, scaled back the extras, and returned to doing the basics well. That decision gave us breathing room. And once we had air again, we could grow on our own terms.

**The Lesson:** Pythons don't crush with speed; they crush with pressure. In business, the same is true. Growth can be good, but unchecked growth can strangle you. The danger isn't only outside corporations; it's in the commitments, distractions, and ambitions that coil around you little by little. The key is vigilance. Know what you can handle, move at a pace you can sustain, and never ignore the warning when you start to feel the squeeze.

Some of the high-impact species, like bees, are essential for maintaining a healthy ecosystem, and some, like the Burmese pythons, cause environmental havoc. It's the same with people. Some are essential for the well-being of your business, but need to be handled carefully, and some need to be kept far away. In the next section, I'll discuss how to create and maintain healthy ecosystems, both out in the world and in your business.

# PART 2

## Creating and Maintaining a Healthy Ecosystem

Most of us understand the need to prevent pollution, consider the effects of our actions on climate change, and work towards maintaining and increasing biodiversity. And we also understand that we need to do the best we can to mitigate the damage already done. This is true at every scale, so we start off with our immediate environment, even just our homes, then expand our circle of concern to the broader community, and ultimately, the whole world. Just like we need a healthy ecosystem in the natural world so we can live and thrive, we need to maintain a healthy business ecosystem through honest business practices, and open and sustainable value chains.

# CHAPTER 5

# Build a Healthy Business

The processes outlined in this book work best if you apply them from day one. Make that day zero. Actually, no, make that day minus a few months or even years. Pre-planning is invaluable. But, if you're already in business and feel that you're surrounded by pestilential people, don't despair. Just like I can eventually get even the most roach- and rat-infested of premises liveable again, you can repair your existing business. It just takes more time.

## Repair Your Existing Business

If your business is actively struggling, you may need to repair, energize and rejuvenate your workforce. Changing a negative or toxic workplace culture takes a lot of work, time, and effort. If you have problems with certain staff members, deal with them appropriately—you may find some tips in part 1—and wherever possible, fix rather than fire. Firing them should be an absolute last resort because it makes the remaining employees nervous. Even more important, if you feel that some of your suppliers or clients are creating more problems than they're worth, it's time to sanitize your supply chain. Slowly let toxic suppliers and customers go.

Last, but not least, it's never too late to make a fresh start, so even if you've been in business a few years, you can implement some of the advice for starting a business.

## First, Look After Number One

Before starting a business, be sure you know why you're doing it and that it is the right decision for you at this point in your life. I was lucky that I had a good job so I could plan my business from a position of security. That really is the ideal situation, but not everyone is that lucky. There are people out there with marketable skills who just can't find a job, so they end up hustling because they have no choice. And, sometimes, that hustle is successful and takes off. These so-called desperation entrepreneurs may have started their companies because they had no choice, but once they've taken off, some of them have become very successful indeed. If you're in that position, some of the foregoing advice might not be applicable to you, but— more importantly—I take my hat off to you. Starting a business even from a position of security is hard, but I am in awe of anyone who can start a successful company out of desperation.

## Right Decision

Starting a business is a big deal, so make sure you're doing it for the right reasons. Some people get kind of pressured into starting a business by friends. Say, for example, you're a great seamstress, potter, or baker, your friends might say, "Wow, that dress/vase/cupcake is better than anything you can buy at the best shops. You should start a business." But don't let the pressure (and perhaps your ego) cloud your judgement. You need more than the core skill to run a business. In fact, the core skill—for example, being able to sew a garment, throw a pot, or bake and ice an awesome wedding cake—is secondary. Some of the most successful restaurants are started and managed by people who can't cook, but they know how to run a business and hire a talented chef.

Entrepreneurship is a state of mind. Quite honestly, I started in the pest control business because that's what my first job was, and I stayed in the industry. If my first job had been as a house painter, I probably would have started a painting business and been just as successful.

Entrepreneurs have a different drive. It's a quest, an ongoing desire to compete. I have a constant desire to win, and there is no limit to what I want to do. I want to constantly succeed. I have clear goals and, as soon as I've accomplished them, I set the next one. They are often very ambitious, but they are always realistic.

I've always had confidence in myself, probably because I've always been realistic. For example, I knew I was cut out to be an entrepreneur because I was confident that I could do this work better on my own than in the company. But I was also realistic, so first I had to put myself in a position to make that step. Jumping in the deep end is all well and good if you can swim, but it's a very silly thing to do if you haven't checked that there's water in the pool. Timing is everything.

## Right Time

I worked for a large company for 30 years before starting my own business. Sure, there were some disadvantages, but they were dramatically outweighed by the advantages. By the time I took that big step, I was extremely ready. I'd actually been ready for a while, but the time had not been right. I'd decided early on that I would not make any major changes to my life until my kids had finished high school. Right from the beginning, I had a date in mind.

Because I'd planned it over the course of a few years, and I'd consulted with my family, I knew I had their support. My wife was 100% behind me, largely because she, too, was confident that I had planned it all properly and wasn't stepping out onto a rickety high board for a deep dive into a pool that may or may not have water in it.

I also knew it was the right time, because I had the funds I'd saved up, instead of borrowing from a bank, for this moment. And, wow, it's a great feeling starting a business knowing you have sufficient capital to keep you going until the business starts showing a profit.

I was also lucky (or perhaps smart) because I was starting a business in an industry that I knew well, was consistent, and was virtually recession-proof. I started from a strong position. But I still had a lot of work to do, so I had to be methodical.

## Make A Plan And Stick To It

And I was methodical. I planned every aspect of the business before I'd even given notice that I was retiring from my corporate job. I was self-funded, I had a start date, and I had worked out that I needed 120 days to get into operation. I planned to leave my job on a specific date—November 05, 2009. I'll never forget that date. I gave my employer 30 days notice because I wanted to leave on good terms and maintain a good relationship.

By doing it in this organized way I felt at ease. I had the capital I needed, and I'd worked out a detailed timeline. But I still had to do an awful lot of fussy admin before I could get going.

There really is a lot of red tape in starting a new business. I had to establish an LLC (a limited liability company) and apply for a business licence. I also had to find premises and buy equipment, and then insure both. In theory, I also had to find staff, but I had all the staff I needed for a start-up: me.

I had my specific retirement date: November 5, 2009. I gave 30 days notice. Then, I took three months off to clear my head. After New Years Day, I had 180 days to get my operation going. By July 15, 2010, Pied Piper was open for business. The break I took was a great idea, because it allowed me to begin feeling relaxed, rested, and strong. I left the starting gate like a racehorse, blazing ahead in the new business.

## Building the Foundation

Those first few heady months were a blur of activity and excitement. I had to implement all my wonderful plans and actually get everything off the drawing board and out into the real world. That involved obtaining equipment and ensuring that the whole business was ethical, safe, sustainable, and practical. It also involved finding people, the bedrock of any organization.

## Create the Dream Team

Businesses get complicated once you start employing people, so I started off as a one-person operation to prove to myself that I could run a business. I was lucky that I had the skills to do my own accounting, because that's not negotiable. If you start off as a one-pony show and you have zero accounting skills, farm it out to a professional. Seriously, you need to do this from day one.

Fortunately, the business grew pretty quickly, and I signed on my first employee after seven months. And that was an interesting experience for me. I'd worked in senior management, so I'd employed, onboarded, and—sadly—fired quite a few people. But doing it for myself was different. While I knew that I had to hire someone for my current needs, I also had to have a long-term view because I didn't want a big staff turnover. I chose people with an eye to long-term development, including hiring a junior tech or office assistant just starting out in their career because they seemed to have management potential. But it was just that—potential. I got it wrong a few times, but I got it right more often. I'm pleased to say that I have something close to my dream team.

## Stay Safe

Whatever business you're in, the health and safety of you, your employees, and your clients is paramount. This is not negotiable. As a pest control professional, I work with chemicals, some of which are toxic, I sometimes encounter hazardous animals, and—perhaps riskiest of all—I drive many miles in all kinds of weather and traffic conditions. I take appropriate precautions for all these different risk scenarios.

In our industry, personal protective equipment (PPE) is essential. Wearing respiratory equipment, protective coveralls, hard hats, and protective boots can be physically tiring and stressful, especially in hot weather.

But having the equipment is no good if you don't use it, and even using it is of little benefit if you don't use it properly. In some circumstances, improperly employed PPE may be more dangerous than none. It is essential that PPE fits properly, is not damaged in any way, and is regularly cleaned. Ill-fitting or damaged PPE can allow dangerous chemicals in and then trap them, and reusing the same PPE without washing it can also end up spreading toxins rather than containing them. More complex safety equipment, like respiratory equipment, needs to be regularly checked and serviced.

What all this means is that, in our industry, you need a strict protocol for PPE use. We require all field staff to wear the appropriate PPE when working, to demonstrate they know how to use it, and to check, clean, maintain, service, and replace their PPE regularly. We also, obviously, require that they obey all the rules of the road and wear safety belts when driving to and from clients. We require this, and we make it clear to all staff, but we can't force them to comply. We can check that the PPE is in the vehicle when the tech leaves, but we can't check that it doesn't stay in the vehicle while they're working.

Ultimately, each staff member must take responsibility for their own safety.

As a manager of a small company, you need to ensure that you have protective systems in place to ensure both your company's sustainability and your employees' safety. The best way to do this is to create and implement good processes. It's also essential that your middle and junior management teams ensure those processes are strictly followed. In his book, *Managing the Risks of Organizational Accidents*, James Reason explains a helpful concept using his Swiss cheese model: Each management level is like a layer of PPE, and you can think of each layer of PPE as a slice of Swiss cheese. It's good and it's solid, but it has holes in it. However, if you layer enough slices of cheese, the holes get covered up.

## Create a Healthy Work Environment

Ensure your employees are safe and secure by creating a healthy physical environment and keeping the premises clean. I make it clear to my staff that maintaining a safe and hygienic work environment is a group effort. Make sure that there is always a comfortable, healthy environment by having windows that allow natural light and installing an efficient HVAC system. Choose a safe location for your business, and ensure that staff and clients can commute, park, and access the building safely. Make sure that the parking area and the approach to the building are well lit. If necessary, use security systems and cameras, which I strongly recommend. In the same way that there is no point in having state-of-the-art PPE sitting in a closet, there's no point in creating a healthy work environment if your employees are not able to take full advantage of it due to safety issues that become apparent before they even enter the building.

## Keep Your Team in Tip-Top Shape

Ensure that your workforce is healthy, well cared for, and happy. The absolute basic minimum is to pay a fair wage, but your responsibility does not end there. Accommodate your staff's need for family responsibility time so they can deal with both foreseen and unforeseen issues with children, spouses, parents, and other family members. Consider adjusted work hours to meet family commitments because football practices, dance recitals, or baby sonograms are important. Most importantly, create an environment in which discrimination and harassment cannot flourish. You do this by setting up systems that operate like a PPE for the office.

Of course, your employees are adults who make their own decisions, but it is worth nudging them towards healthier choices. Make healthy lunch and snack choices available by keeping a fruit bowl in the office so that workers can grab an apple for free instead of buying a chocolate bar when they feel the need for something sweet. Or stock the fridge with bottled water and other healthy drink options. You could also offer subsidized gym membership or encourage teams to have walk-and-talk meetings in a nearby park. A simple thing like having showers in the building can encourage employees to cycle, run, or walk to work. The operative word is "encourage" because putting pressure on employees to conform to an externally imposed lifestyle can create stress. Most important of all, put processes in place to let your employees know that they are valued.

Your business extends beyond the confines of your office, factory, or premises. To ensure your workforce remains happy and healthy, you need to situate your business within a broader healthy ecosystem. Choose your suppliers and customers well. Create a responsible, sustainable supply chain, and create and maintain relationships based on mutual trust and respect. Pay creditors promptly, and charge consistent fair prices.

## Stay Sustainable

When I started my business, I was careful with money because, quite honestly, I had to be. I was, obviously, tempted to order a range of gorgeous, professional-looking branded uniforms but I was realistic. I bought four shirts from the Goodwill Store and embroidered my logo on them. And there's nothing wrong with blue jeans.

And my first truck? I went to a company that sold used leased vehicles, because I knew that leased vehicles were well maintained, and purchased a 2-year-old 2008 Dodge truck that had been owned by a competitor. It served me well, started every time, gave me no trouble, and sold for more than I'd paid for it when I eventually let it go in 2025.

I did the same with property. I started off in rented premises I had sublet from a beauty salon, but, only nine months into the lease, the person we were renting from evicted us so she could let the space to a masseuse. I had to find new premises, and I did not want to put myself in this position again. Although the business was doing well, it was still early days. I didn't want to waste money by renting, so I decided to buy. I used to drive past an abandoned gas station, which I thought would make great premises. So I went to City Hall to get the name and phone number of the owner. I called many times over two or three days but with no reply. There was nowhere I could lease and nowhere I could buy, so I did get a bit disheartened. But then something told me to check my CRM for that person's name, and it popped up in my computer system. The phone number was different. They answered, met with me, and agreed to sell because they "really like Robert," the pest control tech who'd been handling their account. I also had to give them free pest control for the rest of their lives. It was worth it. That property, and the ones I've bought since, have made sure that I'll be comfortable into my old age.

I strongly recommend buying premises rather than renting if you possibly can. I worked hard to pay off the first building, and then rented it back to the business. Then I used that rental income to buy another building, which I paid off in about three years. And then I did the same again. I keep the property portfolio separate from Pied Piper and rent the buildings out to the company. This really is a great strategy that not only gives you cost-effective premises to work from, but is a great investment in its own right. It can also be very satisfying. Six years after I'd been evicted from the beauty parlor building, it came up for sale. I bought it and evicted the beautician who'd evicted me.

I can't emphasize this enough: Spend what you absolutely have to; don't stint on good equipment, good products, targeted marketing, insurance, and good management processes like accounting. But don't go wild on unnecessary marketing, branding, smart office furniture, and fancy vehicles. Watch the money that comes in, watch the money that goes out, and don't spend more than you earn. But more about that in chapter 7.

Now that you've created a safe, healthy, pest-free work environment, you need to make sure it stays that way by putting in place systems to prevent reinfestation.

# CHAPTER 6

# Future-Proof Your Business

You've put a lot of time, effort, and money into setting up a healthy business ecosystem, so now you need to ensure it stays healthy and viable, by proactively creating strategies for dealing with change and developments, both expected and unexpected.

## Protect Your Image

Your staff are a walking billboard for your company, so make sure they look the part. Pied Piper supplies everything our employees wear externally—pants, shirts, shoes, belts, and hats—and we replace them on an ongoing basis at no cost to the employee.

I know there are companies out there who put limits on how many clothing items they pay for in a year, because they want their employees to "look after" their uniforms, but I don't. I want my staff to work hard, knowing that if they tear a shirt or a pair of pants, it will be replaced at company expense. And, as soon as any item starts looking a bit old or tatty, we replace them, because I don't want my staff out there in a faded or threadbare shirt. Or even worse, a stained one. And we don't give away any old branded clothing. We cut up old hats and shirts and throw them away, because I don't want anything with my logo being worn by anyone I would not be proud to have as an employee.

## Pest-Proofing

In the same way that you need to guard against reinfestation once you've treated a premises for pests, there are some safeguards you need to put in place to make sure your business stays healthy and productive. You need to sanitize your business and your supply chain, and put in place a protocol of checking to make sure that pests don't creep in.

### Watch Out for Bloodsucking Vampires And Thieves

Guard against staff sucking your resources by establishing well-defined processes with checks and balances. This is especially important for employees who are paid by the hour or who earn commission. You need to ensure that every order, every invoice, and every receipt balance to ensure that salespeople are not padding accounts, or even creating fictional ones, and that vehicle logs and time sheets concur. Call every client after the service to make sure they're happy.

I make a point of doing quality control check-ins by phoning the client and finding out if anything went wrong and what went right. If all is good, I use the call as an opportunity to ask for a review. I make a point of doing these no later than two days after the service.

You also need to guard against thieves and bandits who might be brazenly helping themselves to equipment or supplies that "fell off the back of your truck." They often work in cahoots with the bloodsuckers, so ensure that your checks and balances also include inventory, deliveries, and equipment maintenance.

Before I started Pied Piper and was still working in corporate, we color-coded the trucks to keep track of equipment. For example, all the hand tools on one truck would be blue, pink, green, yellow, orange, or whatever. That way, if one of the techs was quietly walking off with the tools from their truck, they couldn't just replace them with someone else's.

If you do have a potential freeloader on your staff, they may find a way to circumvent your system of checks and balances, so update them constantly. Take advantage of technology to implement your checks, but carefully. If you don't understand what the tech is doing, you can't check that it's doing its job properly, and you will be at the mercy of the people who do.

## Watch Out for Underminers and Assassins

Protect yourself from passive aggressive employees who undermine the business by doing the bare minimum to not get themselves fired. They're often so skilled and sneaky you won't know what's happening until it's too late. Totally different, but equally dangerous are the workers who design and/or refine systems so much that they are the only people who understand them, and then they hide in the back room, like a scorpion under a rock, quietly making sure everything works perfectly. But, when they leave, everything falls apart, because no one else can understand the byzantine systems they've put in place. Create your own ecosystem and keep abreast of any changes or new processes. Keep it simple, so that almost anyone in the company can take over. You can't build a business around one person who holds the "keys to the kingdom."

For example, termite initial treatments are 10% of Pied Piper's business, and we have one main person who deals with it, but it would be a mistake to not have other techs who also understand the treatment process. Anyone can get sick, and if a long-standing client asks for termite control the week that our termite guy is sick or injured, we could lose them. Always make sure that at least two staff members can do any one particular job.

The key to ensuring that you don't fall prey to the nasty people-pests described above is clear, open, and honest communication. And that works for your supply chain as well—upstream and downstream, suppliers and customers. Because suppliers and customers can also be pesky.

## Communicate Clearly

You also need to have well-constructed contracts with your suppliers, specifying quality, quantity, price, and delivery dates. It's also important to clearly understand exactly who you are doing business with, because if you have an intermediary and there is an issue with delivery or quality, you could end up being pushed from one to the other. So make sure you know exactly which company is responsible for delivering your equipment and supplies, and hold them accountable. If they have a problem with their suppliers, that's their problem, not yours.

Your clients are the lifeblood of your business, so make sure they know exactly what to expect from you and what is expected of them. Some service businesses do not draw up pre-service contracts, but I always do. That way, the client knows what they're getting and what they're paying. The service tech knows exactly what they are supposed to do and what is not in scope. So if the client sweetly asks them to "just quickly also do X, Y, Z, while you're here," the tech has the ammunition to say no. Of course—and this is really important—my techs have been properly trained to upsell and cross-sell, in which case they get commission.

The best way to communicate clearly is in writing. I had a client who complained after a service that pests were found in a shrink-wrapped pallet they had shipped to one of their clients, and they were going to have to credit the client and pay the cost of returning the shipment. But then I brought out the signed pre-service contract, and they had specifically excluded that area from the service. Contracts protect both parties. If we had not performed the service as outlined in the contract, the client would have had the right to expect some form of reparation; however, in this case, it protected us, because it showed that we had provided the service as agreed. But we had fallen short of the level of service I like to give. We'd been servicing the company for years, and everything had always been fine, but they'd recently employed a new plant manager, who we had never met. And this manager did not understand that it was not enough to only treat the part of the premises where the problem was visible. We dropped the ball there. The CSR (customer service representative) who'd taken the order should have queried the client more about why they only wanted part of the premises serviced and not the rest. But they didn't because we'd been blindsided by an unexpected change of management. It was a learning experience, a lesson to not assume that things are as they've always been. Change is the only constant, so we should expect it.

## Expect the Unexpected

The unexpected staff change in the above story could have been a problem, but it wasn't because we had a system in place to deal with issues like that. Staff turnover can be quite high in some of our clients' and suppliers' businesses, and the ramifications can be serious.

### What Happens When a Decision Maker Changes?

I just lost a $25,000-a-year contract because of staff changes. The purchasing officer of one of our long-standing clients retired, and when the new incumbent inadvertently left us off the bid list, a different company won the bid. I had come to rely on the client to send the bid request, and I did not follow up when it didn't arrive. Big mistake.

It was particularly hard losing this client because we'd worked hard over the years to get their premises to a point where the servicing was just low-key maintenance with very few problems. It was more profitable than it had been in the first few years. I sort of feel a bit like someone else harvested the field that I so carefully plowed and sowed. It was an expensive lesson, and I have now invested in a person to check up on existing clients on a regular basis.

## COVID-19

The COVID-19 pandemic certainly caught me by surprise—along with the rest of the world. We were not mentally prepared for COVID, but pest control is resilient to recession, so we didn't do too badly. We were considered an essential service and could continue working. We had one major advantage over many other businesses in that we were used to wearing masks and gloves, but we still had to adapt. For example, we concentrated more on exterior applications wherever possible, and we had to fine-tune our email and phone communication. And ensuring a reliable supply of PPE was tricky, because all of a sudden, we had lots of other buyers vying for a limited supply. In fact, we had such a good supply that we were in a position to supply some of our bigger customers early on. We did this free of charge, which really helped to entrench customer loyalty.

The big lesson I learned from Covid is that, in business, you do not know what's going to be handed to you. Always expect the unexpected. A leader's calm in chaos isn't born from knowing the outcome—it's forged in refusing to flinch when no one else can see the road.

## Financial Sustainability

I've discussed the importance of good financial systems, and I don't mind repeating it here, because that cannot be emphasized too much. Rule Number 1 is to spend less than you earn, and Rule Number 2 is to keep track of every penny spent and earned, because that's the only way you can ensure that you don't break Rule Number 1. Don't overspend on nonessentials, but don't skimp on essentials, like good equipment, good supplies, good staff, realistic marketing, and—so easy to skimp on—appropriate-level insurance.

## Insurance—the Essential Safety Net

Don't overinsure, because you'll never get that money back, and don't underinsure, because that can come back to bite you when you need to claim. Find a good insurance agent who will shop the market and help you figure out the best level of insurance as the business grows. Don't make the mistake of insuring accurately at the beginning, and then not upping the value of your cover as the business grows. Also, don't skimp on liability insurance, but again, don't go crazy insuring yourself to the hilt. I used to have only $2 million dollars liability insurance, which was fine until I tendered for a contract that required $3 million dollars insurance. No problem—I bid for the job, and only when I was awarded the contract, did I up my insurance.

Another important aspect of ensuring you get the best cover for the best price is to carefully manage your risk profile. For example, when employing a new tech, I always check their driving record. I don't want someone who regularly gets into fender benders driving one of my trucks and ruining my claims record. On that subject, I know of some business owners who insure their family cars under the business. That's not a good idea if you have teenage kids who regularly hit the gatepost turning into the driveway, or who "just scrape" other cars while imperfectly parallel parking.

Insurance is not just a good idea, it's also a legal requirement. You really can't get away with not having it. But what about ensuring the stability of the business? There's no law about that. Now, as I look in the mirror, I see less and less grey hair, but that's not because it isn't grey. It's all grey, but there seems to be a bit less of it every day, and that got me thinking.

## Succession Planning

We all think we're going to live forever, but sometimes we get a rude reminder of the fact that we're mortal. It may be a health scare, the sudden death of a friend or family member, or maybe a fender bender that we realize could have been worse. Whatever the inciting incident, it's a reminder that we need to put our affairs in order. And that includes our business affairs. If you're a small business owner, you need to think long and hard about what will happen if you leave your home one morning and don't make it to the office. How will the business keep going? Will the staff get paid at the end of the month? If your estate is in probate for months or even, as is more likely, years, what will happen to the business?

This is a tough discussion but it's one that needs to happen. But before you share your plans and/or concerns with your staff, start by discussing these issues with your spouse and possibly other family members. Do it now, while you're still hale and hearty, not on your deathbed.

A few years ago, after I had just such a wake-up call, I restructured all my business holdings to ensure they can continue seamlessly if I were to drop off the end of the earth tomorrow.

I've drafted a living will and set up a living trust, which took six months to do, and it was not cheap, but that's not the point. The benefit is I could go back to my leadership team and explain to them exactly what to do, how to keep the business running, and how to ensure staff, suppliers, and clients can rest assured that they will be paid and serviced as before. If you've created a genuine family business, you probably think you don't need to do that because you are already grooming your children (or child) to take over. I don't want to sound like a doomsayer, but don't be too sure about that. Unless they are totally committed, you may one day find that they've nurtured a secret dream of running a backpacker's lodge in Bali or teaching scuba diving in the Seychelles, and they just haven't told you because you never really asked. You assumed.

## Passive Income

I explained in chapter 5 that, after a very short time renting, I bought the first property for the business, and three years later once it was paid off, I bought another. I've made a bit of a habit of this, so I now have a sustainable revenue stream from a very nice commercial property portfolio to bolster the pest control earnings. I created a new LLC called Pied Piper Holdings that owns and manages the properties and rents them out to Pied Piper Pest & Lawn and other businesses. I'm not planning on retiring for a while, but when I do, I will keep an interest in the holding company that owns the properties so that I can have a dependable retirement income.

# CHAPTER 7

# Living and Working in Balance

When you run a small business in the service sector, you soon learn how interconnected everything is and how important it is to maintain an equilibrium. You need to balance work and life, you should be sound in mind, body, and finances, and you need to cultivate good and lasting relationships along your entire value chain. It does require some juggling skill, so you need to stay on top of things, which requires good physical and mental health, and sound communication strategies. Work–life balance isn't a scale you manage—it's a heartbeat you protect. When it skips too long for work, life forgets its rhythm.

## Body

In chapter 5, I discussed ways that you can encourage your staff to adopt a healthier lifestyle, but there's no point having healthy employees if you're not up to the job yourself. Like it or not, it's essential to regularly check your blood pressure, cholesterol, and other vitals that require invasive tests we don't enjoy. Also, depending on the industry you're in, you may need a certain level of fitness, strength, and flexibility. And, perhaps, a head for heights.

I believe in leading from the front. I wouldn't ask my employees to do something I'm not prepared to do, so you may well find me 30 feet off the ground in a bucket lift or crawling around in tight, termite-infested spaces. It's tough and it gets tougher the older you get, so staying in good shape is essential. But staying in physical shape is no use if you don't pay attention to your mental and emotional well-being.

## Mind

After 30 years in corporate, the last 15 years running my own business have flown by. Every day has been a challenge, but in a good way. Some days, I've had the luxury of sitting back and seeing the big picture, but most days I've had to focus on specifics. And when you do that, you can lose track of time, and if you lose track of time, you can lose track of what is important.

On a personal note: I've learned to appreciate the quiet times when it seems that nothing is happening. Just because it's quiet doesn't mean that business is dead. It means all your bees are out in the flower fields. No buzz is not necessarily bad. Enjoy it. In fact, I find those quiet times so productive that after I'd been running my own business, I moved my private office to another building.

It's important to do this at the right time. Some business owners do it too soon. I had to develop the team to the level where I could leave and feel great about it. It took me nine years of working day-to-day with my team to move down the road. A lot of business leaders leave before fully preparing themselves and the team. And that's where the business begins to fail because no one's there. As much as we'd like to believe it, service businesses don't run on auto-pilot.

Another thing that enables me to fully focus when I am at work is a healthy boundary between business, family, and community. I like every one of my employees: I enjoy working with them, and I care about their general well-being, which includes their families and their lives outside the office. But I keep healthy boundaries. When I socialize with staff, it's at the office or in a neutral space. This is good for my work life, my productivity, the productivity of my staff, and my home life. My lovely wife knows that when I am at home, I am at home. I am a husband, not a business owner.

Also, as the staff I've brought on has grown with the company to the point where I can delegate, I can spend more time on high-level management, which requires a little distance. Of course, you can create this by simply closing your door, but I've chosen to move my personal office to give me more space. And I'm lucky that I can.

## Space

As I outlined in chapter 5, I started Pied Piper in rented premises and bought more suitable premises as soon as it was financially viable. That put the business in a sufficiently comfortable position to enable me to continue to expand the company's real estate portfolio. About six years ago, I bought and renovated an abandoned building that had been converted at the turn of the century to horse stables attached to the first bank in town. Yes, there was a time when every bank needed its own stables. Life must have been simpler then, but as a pest control professional, I shudder to think of the fly issues with the stables right next to the bank. All that aside, once the renovations were complete, I moved my private office from the main premises to the new building. It's only about half a mile away, so I can be at the premises in almost no time if necessary, but mentally, it's in another space entirely. Of course, this could entail extra expense, but as I will explain a bit later, it could also be an added benefit of a financially sound business decision. In my case, it was the latter, and the move has been positive in every way. It's given me the space—literally—to concentrate on strategy while the rest of the team goes about their day-to-day business knowing that I trust them to do it well. And they do.

Being slightly removed from the hustle and bustle gives me the space to concentrate on strategy instead of day-to-day tasks. If I feel my mind wondering, I become worked up about something, or I can't concentrate, I simply lay my phone down on my desk, open the door, and take a stroll around the block. It's just a 15- or 20-minute break, but it allows me to clear my thoughts and clear my head. Just take a mental break, basically putting myself in timeout. Adult timeout.

Another advantage of having my office in this separate location is that one of the other "tenants" is my wife, who operates her quilting business from another office in the same building. Some people believe their marriage is improved by long daily absences, and I understand that perspective, but I like having her nearby. We're both busy during the day, so we hardly see each other, but it gives me a sense of security knowing she's close by. I like to think she feels the same way. After all, we all need community.

## A Balanced and Well-Structured Team

Just like a business, a garden is also an ecosystem of sorts, and any gardener can tell you that you don't plant roses in the shade. And it's the same with your staff. Be careful when promoting people that you don't move them out of the metaphorical sun where they are thriving into the shade where they will wither and die. If you have someone who is a technical genius but not great with people, don't promote them to a managerial position. You'll just make everyone miserable. But, if your business is growing, you have to keep your staff growing. You absolutely cannot do everything yourself, so you need staff, particularly management staff. And that can be hard. If you started a business from scratch, it's hard to let go of the reins and trust your baby to someone else. So you need people you trust.

### Nurturing Your Team

I think of my support staff as just that—support. I still take responsibility, but I certainly don't want to micromanage. And the way I ensure I don't have to is by careful, consistent training. This is especially important with new technology, procedures, or equipment.

Regardless of how long they've been in the business, I start the training by outlining how things were done in the past.

Then I explain why we changed and describe how things are done now. Then I make sure they can perform the task to the required level. I understand that some managers may think the first two steps are not necessary, but I think they are.

I believe you get more of a buy-in if you explain why things are done the way they are, because if employees understand why they're doing something that way, they will remember it. It also reduces the likelihood that they will try to change the new process, because they've been shown what doesn't work.

I've found that my best workers are people who joined the company as juniors and worked their way up with me. Not least, probably, because they tend to do things the way I like because that's how they learned. I've invested time in them, and I find the more you add to the investment, the more return you get. It doesn't have to be a lot at a time. It can be just a few minutes a week. It's a layering effect. You'll notice your employees getting better and better with each positive reinforcement, with each new skill learned. You can even check in with employees virtually, but it is nice to have a face-to-face once or twice a month as well.

## Be Creative

I mentioned that I've embraced AI, but only in specific situations. I've created an AI assistant that can help technicians in the field by, for example, confirming the dilution ratio of a specific chemical or working out whether they can use a specific chemical in, for example, a food processing facility. This really saves time, but it's not magic. It's a tool, and it is only as good as the information it's been fed. But that's okay, because

I fed it good information. I believe AI is going to be huge in our industry, and I intend to be on the forefront and take full advantage of it.

## Be Supportive

We are constantly working on our ecosystem because I believe in constant improvement and growth. I encourage my staff to enroll in continuing education programs. Knowledge is power, so we offer to help people with college tuition, as long as it is relatively useful. It doesn't have to be in a strictly related field, like entomology or chemistry, but it must be useful. A business degree? Yes. Accounting? Yes. HR? Yes. Ancient history? Probably not. We evaluate each case individually so, depending on what the employee wants to study, we might provide full or partial tuition payment,) and we will give them time off for study.

## But Don't Be a Pushover

It really is important to be caring and understanding, especially if an employee is facing some kind of personal issue, like illness, a death in the family, or other challenges. But some people just can't resist taking advantage if they think you're going to be soft. So don't.

I had an employee who was repetitively late, so I compared his handwritten report to the GPS on his truck, and found an average discrepancy of about 30 minutes a day. That adds up to 2.5 hours a week, and he was paid hourly. Clearly, that was a problem, so now I make sure that someone compares the GPS readings with the report for every tech every day. It's added work for one employee, and added cost for the company, but it probably pays for itself. And I'm pleased to say that, after some intervention, he changed his ways and is now a model employee.

## Community

Your business is a community, and it is in a community. You can almost think of it like those Russian nesting dolls. The inner community is you and your closest confidantes. Just outside of that is your employees and their families, then your suppliers and customers, and then the broader community—your neighborhood, town, state, and even country.

Your business exists within a broader community, and your supply chain is a delicate thread that can be broken at any point. Or reinforced at any point. Always keep a lookout for ways you can strengthen ties with your clients and suppliers—and your community, because your community is filled with potential clients and potential suppliers.

### Close Confidantes

You need someone close to you that you trust, who can raise a flag, and when they do, you need to listen. In my case, it's my lovely wife of 44 years. But we really only spend time together when I'm home. She knows my overall health and the deepest, darkest secrets of my soul, but I also need a more pragmatic day-to-day confidante. I have a co-manager, Terry, who has worked with me for over 30 years, and I value his guidance. He is very honest with me, which is great, because we all need someone to keep us on track and let us know if we're losing the vision. I'm pretty sure that, unlike my wife, Terry does not love me unconditionally, but he understands the business that we're in, so we speak the same language. We want the same thing, ultimately. We're on the same team.

## Peer Decompression

I've joined a business peer group with nine other pest control and lawn care business owners. We chat on a regular basis about business concerns. Those closed discussions are great. It's nice to be able to talk about common issues, concerns, and business struggles. It's a great way to exchange great ideas and useful information. It's called Alpha, and we're mostly all alpha dogs, so there are no holds barred and no punches pulled. But it's all in good faith, and it's all genuinely positive. Sometimes, you just need to hear the truth from someone who sits in the same chair you do every day. I'm sure there are similar groups for other industries, so look around.

## Broader Community

One of the advantages of being a small, local business is that you can use innovative marketing strategies that capitalize on your being part of that community. For example, I've partnered up with local schools and presented a program, called "Good Bug, Bad Bug" for kids in the 2nd, 3rd, and 4th grades. They love it, and it provides useful information on how to identify beneficial insects and explain why they are good. Of course, I also teach them how to identify problem pests—the squirmy little troublemakers nobody wants around but kids love to hate. I give them a goodie bag with branded coloring books and other promotional items at the end. I used to include fly swatters, but the parents and teachers asked me not to, because they were used more against other children than against flies.

I guess I'm lucky that pest control lends itself to this kind of program, but be creative with your own industry. If you run a plumbing service, you could give workshops on water saving. If you run a gardening service, you could discuss growing vegetables or the secret language of flowers. Hopefully, some of the people in these broader communities will become customers, and your customers are your most important community.

## Customers

In the service industry, the customer is king, queen, or whatever word you would use to denote "very important." Without customers, you have no business, so customer service and communication should be your top priority. And they are intimately linked. Our service begins before the tech arrives at the client's premises, and it does not end when they drive away in their truck. We follow up every call.

### Follow-up

We phone the client after every service to find out how the call went. If there's an issue, we will fix it the same day or the day after. No later. And here's where employee trust and agency are important. My CSRs are empowered to do whatever it takes to make up for any dissatisfaction. They don't call me to get my permission to give a credit, go back for a free follow-up, or even both.

If we sense that the client is 100% happy, we may ask for a review, and send them a link to make it easy, but the main reason for the call is genuinely to check that they received good service. The review is secondary. And, while we have them on the phone, we also mention our referral program. We offer them a $25 credit for every referral.

Losing a client is bad. I measure growth in number of customers, not in increased revenue, so I analyze the client data for number of customers rather than cash value at the end of every month, quarter, or year. And, if I lose a customer, I try to find out why. I track lost clients by technician and take action to improve service. My first choice would be to upskill the technician, but if that doesn't work, I'll replace them in a heartbeat.

**Transparency and Honesty**

I believe that quality of service is more important than price, but nothing is more important than consistent, honest communication. So our pricing is consistent. We have an established pricing guide based on square footage, and that doesn't change. What that means is that when someone phones, our CSR can give them a definite, final price as long as their square footage is accurate. They don't have to check, ask, or get permission for anything. It's quick and simple. We automatically increase our price every year, by no less than 5%. And we include this notification in our service agreement.

**Potential Customers**

Almost every business owner can tell you their profit. They can always tell you their revenue, but can they tell you how many customers they have? I can. And, because I measure my growth by the number of customers, I am always actively looking for new ones.

I researched my competition until I knew them better than they knew themselves. If I have a new client, I check to see who their last service provider was. I have a stash of copies of past contracts from most of my competitors. I target their clients, so I can improve on their service by identifying the gaps in their service offering. Sometimes, if I'm bidding for a big client, I may show them my competitor's contracts.

Knowledge is power, but not power just for the sake of power. I use that knowledge to find out what my clients really need and then offer a better service. And, yes, I use my competitors' contracts to improve mine, because contracts are the basis of the client–service provider relationship. Contracts are everything.

## Contracts

Some customers, especially large commercial customers, are very specific about what they want. I am the guardian of their ecosystem, so I write a scope of service that explains exactly how I'm guarding that ecosystem. That's the trust. If they want to modify or change it, they can, but there will be a cost. If you don't have an agreement with the client, how do you know what to do, and how do they know they've got what they want and need? I have competitors who pride themselves on not using contracts and even advertise "no contracts." I think that's crazy. Contracts are good. This is what you hang your hat on.

Contracts protect both parties by carefully outlining the scope, service, and price. A contract is a simple document that explains what you will do, when you will do it, how you will do it, and what it will cost. It also includes a warranty that protects the client in the case of substandard service. More important from my perspective, though, is that it protects me as well—as I described in the previous chapter. In that instance, the contract made it clear that any damages suffered by the client were because they had chosen to ignore our advice. That showed just how important communication is, and it is even more important for clients who require special services.

## Special Needs Clients

One day, the maintenance director of a hospital called me in a state of alarm. A patient had brought bedbugs into the emergency room, so it had to be inspected and possibly treated. Now, treating an emergency room with any form of an insecticide requires significant planning, preparation, and special precautions. Together with the hospital staff, we prepared a service protocol for the areas that could be serviced and discussed strategies, such as heat treatments and deep cleaning, for those that could not. Once the standard operating procedure (SOP) had been approved by all the department heads, we formulated a master scope of service. Once the approval was received, which was within a few hours, we provided the required treatments within the set time windows, and the overall service was a success.

A few days later, we invited all the department heads to a meeting at the hospital. We sponsored snacks and drinks and presented our bedbug protocol program to the entire group. This session helped us to identify a downstream lack of knowledge. So we developed a bedbug training program for ER techs, nursing staff, and other staff. It covered how to identify bedbugs, the bedbug lifecycle, and what to do if they are found. Now we do regular in-service training days for the hospital, taking about two hours for each department. I've also produced a tailor-made training manual for staff to keep on hand and consult whenever necessary.

We didn't charge them for this, but the benefits are huge. Empowering the staff with knowledge means they don't phone us every time they see a ground beetle and, even more important, the hospital employees feel better about their jobs. Knowledge is power. It's hard to put a value on this, both for us and for the hospital. It's also hard to put a value on our working relationship. What I can say, though, is that every year when I increase the contract by 8% or 10%, they smile and sign without hesitation.

Also, if any of the management or staff have a pest problem, who will they call? Sorry, there are no prizes for answering this question right because it's just too easy.

The real value, though, is in the results. Misidentification dropped, and—initially—bedbug calls increased because they were finding the evidence sooner. That means the level of infestation was smaller, so the job was easier and more profitable. And there was less follow-up work. It really is a win-win-win situation. The hospital has less bedbugs (always a good thing), so the patients have a better experience, the staff are happier and more confident, and I get less work for much the same financial return. I've done similar programs for hotel staff, and I will gladly craft a special course for any industry.

This level of communication is what differentiates superb service from okay service. By having my ear to the ground and listening to the customer, I learned how I could help them more. It was more than a simple bedbug control service. I worked out what they needed to know and empowered their staff, so it was more about how we did it rather than just what we did. And the end result is better pest prevention. Truly, a win-win-win.

## Business Flexibility and Agility

In a natural ecosystem, a plant or animal that is too specialized may go extinct in the face of change. Take the Australian koala bear or the giant panda, for example. The koala lives only on eucalyptus leaves and the panda primarily on bamboo. If either of these plants were to be wiped out by, say, a bamboo aphid or eucalyptus blight, these vulnerable creatures would follow suit pretty quickly. It's the same in business. You need a niche, you need to specialize, and you need well-defined systems, but you also need to be flexible—ready to change tack at a moment's notice to survive a threat or take advantage of a new opportunity.

## New Opportunities

Soon after starting Pied Piper, I was servicing a lakeside home, when the owner asked if I did lawn care. With a strong ego, I looked at her and said "no." She asked "Why not?" I did not have an answer, but after I'd pondered it for a while, I realized it was a good question. I went home and it just troubled me. For days after that, even weeks, as I thought about it, I realized it would not take much to get into that part of the business. I repeated her question to myself, "Why not?"

One of my existing chemical suppliers also sold herbicides and fertilizers, so he came out and showed me the ropes. I cross-trained one of my existing employees, retooled an existing truck for the lawn market, and began our quest into lawn care. I'm so glad I swapped my knee-jerk "No" response for a flexible and constructive inquisitiveness. Instead of "No," I said "Why not?" Lawn care is now 30% of our revenue, millions of dollars.

I often think back to that encounter. I did get her as a lawn customer, but I got so much more as well. I learned invaluable lessons that have stood me in good stead ever since.

The first was to always be attentive to your customer's needs. Do they have a pain you can fix? You never know when that need may present an opportunity. Remember, Need = Opportunity!

Second, think long and hard about any way you can cross-service. If you are a plumber already installing baths and showers, maybe you should add a tiler to your team.

Last, and most importantly, when faced with a new idea, new concept, or new opportunity, always ask **"Why not?"**

I think that simple two-word question might be what sets entrepreneurs apart—an open mind. Entrepreneurs don't wait for permission to build; they start with a question, "Why not?" and then they let possibility draw the blueprint.

## Be Prepared to Think Big

Some business owners don't grow because they have a small mentality and don't believe they can. That's a truly limiting philosophy, so I always consider doing things other people may think are beyond my reach. Granted, after mulling them over, I do realize that some are genuinely beyond my reach, but at least I know why, because I've analyzed the whole scenario.

Even more important, though, is that after careful consideration I often find that I can take on that huge contract. For example, I have a contract with a large paper manufacturing company that's worth hundreds of thousands of dollars; however, when I first saw the opportunity, it seemed too big. For starters, they required $3 million in liability insurance, but I only had $2 million at the time. Well, hey, I realized after very little thought, that's fixable. So I tendered and, when I was awarded the contract, I upped my insurance to $3 million dollars to be compliant. And then, I saw another contract out to tender that required $4 million dollars insurance. I worked out that it would cost me less than $2,000 a year for the extra million in coverage, but the contract would bring in $500,000 a year. No brainer. I did the same thing and upped my insurance when I was awarded the contract.

It's important to note that I never lied or cheated on these tenders. I was genuinely capable of doing the work and the level of coverage was the only constraint. I went ahead with my bid knowing that I could fix that with one phone call to my broker. In these cases, it was insurance, but it could have been equipment or staff. Say, for example, I had everything I needed to confidently bid for a $1 million contract, except for one rather expensive piece of machinery—a $300,000 doodad. Same story: I'd bid for the contract, and if I got it, I'd immediately spend the $300,000 on the doodad, knowing it would bring in $1 million.

It could have been a specialist in some very technical process. Same story. Bid for the job, and if you get it, add the relevant specialist to your team.

Be prepared to think big, and stay flexible so you can dance to a new and exciting tune. The world doesn't remember what you dreamed—it remembers what you built while others were still dreaming.

## Flexible HR

Like I said before, I've been in the pest control business for 45 years, so you can probably guess that I learned to do things back in the day when fax machines were cutting edge technology, the closest thing to a computer anyone dreamed of was a handheld calculator, and carrying a pager made me feel like James Bond. I've had to adapt to new technology as I've grown with the business, and I've even found a truly useful purpose for AI.

More importantly, though, I have been open to learning from a diverse office ecosystem. I left school, got a job, worked hard, made money, and am confidently expecting a comfortable retirement. I confess, I could have spent more time with my family, but I was focused on the goal. That's what my generation did.

I found out several years ago that quality of life and work–life balance is more important for the upcoming generations than the additional money of overtime. It's not that they're lazy, and it's not that they don't care. They do care, and they work hard—when they are at work—but they also play hard, pray hard, sleep hard, socialize hard, or just spend more time with their family. They work in order to fund what they consider important.

Looking back, I realize I did what everyone expected and that, perhaps, I should have been less willing to accept the norm without questioning it. For example, it never occurred to me to take parental leave when my kids were born, but perhaps I would have been a happier father if I had. (I probably would have got some ribbing from the team though.)

I am learning from my staff how to make the work ecosystem comfortable for them. I always have had an employee handbook, and I still have one. It contains a set of policies and procedures I can use to enforce the rules, but I think it may be more important, and ultimately more productive, to keep my eyes and ears open to find new benefits and keep my mind open to change. The needs of staff are constantly evolving, so we update our employee handbook every year.

Ask the bee workers how to make the hive stronger and where the good flowers are. If you ask the question in the right way and take their needs into consideration, you'll find they will reward you with loyalty and good work.

Take, for example, the reluctance to work overtime. That probably would not have worked 45 years ago when I was starting out, but it just requires a slight change of perspective. So, I thought to myself, why insist on eight people working ten hours a day, when I could have ten people working eight hours a day? I'd get the same hours and probably even get more work done in those hours, because each person would have more energy. Even more important, if one of them is sick, I'd have to divide their eight hours of work between nine people, rather than dividing ten hours between seven people.

## Finances

This should almost go without saying, but it's surprising how many otherwise sound new businesses fail because of bad financial planning.

Regardless of how small you are, get an accountant from day one, even if that accountant is you. You want to watch the money, so you don't spend more than you earn. That's the crux, really.

Start with a profit and loss statement, so you can understand what's coming in, what's going out, and what's left over. Track it month after month, year after year, and be prepared for ups and downs. Like a good beekeeper, don't take all the honey. This is the key for me. I put personal desires aside (for a while) and constantly reinvested in the company. I could have paid myself more, but I chose to delay that gratification and reinvested in marketing, an additional staff member, equipment, or another truck. This way, I was giving the company a little hedge against bad times and, even more importantly, ensuring greater and more sustainable growth. So now, after a decade or so of restraint, I can pay myself a good salary, while keeping the business running and growing sustainably. It took some discipline for a few years, but I'm reaping the rewards now.

## Bottom Line

And that's what it's all about. That's why I went into business for myself in the first place. Yes, it was for the job satisfaction, and the freedom to choose how and where I would work, but it was also for security. I started the business from a position of relative security and built it up to be a strong base from which to retire and enjoy the fruits of my labor.

I'm happy to say I've done that successfully, and I could retire tomorrow but I probably won't because I'm still having fun. And that's the real win. Choice. The freedom to choose is the greatest gift you can give yourself.

# CONCLUSION

When I left corporate and started Pied Piper, I brought with me a whole lot of technical and management experience. I knew how to help my clients live a pest-free life in their homes and business premises, and I had also learned how to ensure the new business I was starting would be free of the human "pests" that I'd learned to deal with throughout my career. Of course, as an owner rather than a manager, I met a few more of these pesky humans, but I've also learned how to control them and guard against reinfestation. This book is my attempt to share my experience with you.

Probably the most important lesson I've learned is that you can't control what life gives you, but you can control how you respond, and I've learned to respond with effort, consistency, and respect. As a young adult, I had to take care of my mom after my father died. I also got married at 18, so I did what I had to do to provide for my family. I started working straight out of school, worked hard and smart, and once my kids had started college, I branched out on my own starting Pied Piper. And I've carried that sense of responsibility through every facet of the business.

I take seriously my commitment to ensuring my clients live and work in places that are pest-free and—in some cases—

surrounded by gorgeous green lawns. I also take seriously my commitment to my staff to ensure they work in an environment that is free from pests, both literal and metaphorical. I run a tight ship, where everyone is confident that they will be treated with fairness and respect, and that their well-being and safety is a priority. I believe that happy employees are loyal, and it shows in the level of commitment of my staff. I consider my employees' families to be a part of our extended community, and I'm open to discussing work-related issues with them if they have concerns.

I'm proud to say that after being in business for a while, I've gotten to a point where I am not afraid to share what I know and even my competitors sometimes call me for advice. This made me realize that when you're no longer afraid to help your competition, you've reached a place of completeness, a place of security, and you've become part of a greater community. I'd learned this give-and-take early in my corporate days by being on the receiving end when another manager helped me when I was just starting on my management journey and was struggling a bit. His advice improved my performance, so I was happy to keep the virtuous momentum going by helping a competitor. It's even paid off in the short term because that competitor now refers clients to me if he can't take them on. What goes around truly does come around; it's a win-win for all.

# TAKE THE LEAP

While it may seem like I've emphasized the negative by focusing on pests and how to deal with them, I confess I did it that way because I wanted to share how I've noticed that many people behave the same way as the pests that create a market for my business.

It's obviously not based on any real science, but there's some truth in it. And, more importantly, it's fun. Yes, purpose, integrity, hard work, and discipline are essential, but so is taking time to laugh, to be playful, and to enjoy the fruits of your labor. Focus on business, but don't neglect your family and friends; they are the bedrock of your life. That's another thing I did: I waited until my whole family was at a place where I could confidently make changes, step out, and take some risks. Because there are always risks going into business for yourself. But I hope the advice I've weaved through the stories about bees, scorpions, rats, snakes, and cockroaches will help you create a stable, successful business.

The principles are simple: Plan well, work hard, don't spend more than you earn, reinvest in the business, and treat people like they should be treated. I can't overemphasize the importance of planning. It was likely Benjamin Franklin who said, "If you fail to plan, you plan to fail," and I couldn't agree more. Plan. And then implement your plans, plug holes, do periodic inspection, wear the proper PPE, invest wisely, nurture your community, and plan for the future. There's more out there than you realize, so be brave.

# LEGACY

After more than 40 years in business, I believe that success isn't just about money or buildings. It's about people. It's about the lives you touch, the teams you build, the competitors you help, and the stories that continue long after you're gone. It's balancing ambition with respect and compassion, investing wisely, and focusing on people—staff, clients, and the community in general. Pied Piper grew from that belief—that leadership means lifting others, that planning creates freedom, and that innovation keeps you alive. When I first started working at the age of 18, I was grateful to be given the opportunity to provide for my family, and I am now delighted that I can do the same for other people. I have gotten to the stage where I can choose employees based on character and aptitude, rather than skills. I also understand that this industry is not for everyone, but I still have a good relationship with many former employees. It hurts a bit when people move on, but I am happy when they find a place where they can thrive. We've built something steady, adaptable, and strong enough to share.

I think of Pied Piper as more than a business. It's a part of my life, and it's a path of opportunity for both me and my staff. It's been hard work but it's never been a struggle, and I'm learning something new every day, so I don't intend on retiring soon. It's keeping me active and on top of things. I love the challenge of staying on the cutting edge.

As I explained in chapter 6, I've thought long and hard about my own future and the future of Pied Piper, and I think we've created something of value, something we can be proud of. I'd like to share it, which is why I've decided to move Pied Piper into a franchise model so that, as the company continues to expand, it can become a pathway for others to find their own business and financial freedom. And a big part of my motivation for franchising is to offer my employees the opportunity—at a significantly reduced cost—to go into business for themselves in an industry they know well. It's all part of extending the community. I'm franchising Pied Piper to serve the next generation, because I believe that real leadership isn't about holding the door open—it's about handing someone the keys.

I hope you've enjoyed reading about some of the real and metaphorical pests I've had to deal with over the course of my career, and I hope you find the advice here useful for your own business, whether it's one you've been operating for years or whether it's a brand-new start-up.

I am passionate about helping small service businesses scale and succeed. If you would like to dive deeper into the strategies shared in this book or explore how we can work together, please use the resources below:

- **Speaking & Coaching:** To book a workshop, inquire about keynote speaking, or explore one-to-one business coaching for service industry businesses, visit www.TimWhitt.com

- **Pest Solutions:** For expert insights into the critters we manage every day and the services we provide, visit www.ThePiedPiper.biz

- **Career & Franchise Opportunities:** Interested in joining our team or launching your own location? Learn how to get involved at www.PiedPiperFranchise.com

# ACKNOWLEDGEMENTS

**To my parents, Delmer and Gertrude—**

Though you're no longer here, your fingerprints are on every good thing I've ever built. You gave your all—not just for me, but for our whole family—for me and my two older brothers. You provided what mattered most: love that didn't waver, faith that didn't fold, and a home where God wasn't a Sunday topic—He was the foundation.

You taught us what it looks like to keep going when times are hard, to work with dignity, to treat people right, and to trust God without using faith as an excuse to sit still. You showed me that God is in control—but we still have a part to play. We still have to show up, do the work, carry responsibility, and walk our journey with purpose. That balance—trusting God fully while doing our part faithfully—has guided me more than any business lesson ever could.

**To my wife, Cindy—**
My rock. My sword. My shield.

For 44 years, you've stood between me and the things that would've taken me out—my own stubbornness included. When the days were heavy, you carried more than your share without keeping score. When the decisions got lonely, you stayed close. When the pressure turned up, you didn't flinch—you steadied me. Any strength people see in me has been sharpened and held together by your love, your grit, and your unwavering loyalty. I built a business, but you built the man who could.

You were the steady ground under moving feet—the calm voice when everything felt urgent, the wise pause when I wanted to push harder, faster, louder. You carried the unseen load: the long seasons, the late nights, the early mornings, the worry you never dramatized, and the faith you never loaned out to circumstances. You made home a refuge. You protected what mattered most—our family, our name, our peace—while I chased what I thought mattered most. And when I came home tired, frustrated, or full of noise from the day, you had a way of bringing me back to what's real.

You weren't just my support—you were my standard. You showed me what strength looks like when it's quiet, what courage looks like when nobody applauds, and what loyalty looks like when it's tested. You stood with me through risk, through growth, through setbacks, through the kind of pressure that makes some people quit or turn cold—and you never let me become the worst version of myself. You reminded me—sometimes gently, sometimes with that look—that success without character isn't success at all. If there's any honor in my leadership, any steadiness in my decisions, any decency in how I've tried to treat people, it traces back to you.

**To my mentors, Cecil Rhodes and Ed Phelan—**
Cecil, the Southern "Gentle Giant," you taught me a lesson most people learn too late: profit isn't luck—profit is the result

of proper teams, clear structure, and doing things the right way on purpose. You believed that a business should run like a well-built house—solid foundation, straight framing, and no hidden rot. You taught me that when roles are clear, expectations are written down, numbers are respected, and leaders hold the line, good people can do great work without chaos stealing their energy. You showed me how to think in systems—how to build the kind of structure that outlasts any one person, including the owner.

You also taught me something just as important as process: how to treat people while you build it. You led with calm strength—never loud, never flashy, just steady and sure. You taught me to give credit freely, correct with dignity, and never confuse being in charge with being above anyone. And you taught me to stay gracious, because people you treat well have a way of coming back around—and sometimes they come back to manage you. That truth has saved me more than once.

Ed "Chief "&"Coach"—you were the kind of leader who protected your tribe without hesitation. If your people were threatened, you'd break ground in a heartbeat or go to war if that's what it took. But you also believed in standards, conditioning, and earned confidence—so if the department or project wasn't in shape, you didn't lecture…you made us run a few more laps. You had a way of making people feel safe *and* accountable at the same time—like you'd step in front of the storm for your team, but you'd also make sure they learned how to stand in the wind themselves.

You taught me that leadership isn't a title—it's responsibility in motion. It's showing up early, staying late, and taking the hard conversations so your people don't have to carry fear to work. You modeled what it looks like to defend the culture like it matters, to protect standards like they're sacred, and to never tolerate disrespect—especially toward the people doing the work. You didn't just manage outcomes; you managed trust.

And you taught me that tough love, done right, is a gift. You pushed because you believed. You demanded more because you saw more. You made us sweat the details because you knew the details are what separate a good department from a great one. You taught me that "coach" isn't a nickname—it's a calling: develop the person, not just the performance. Because when a team is conditioned—trained, disciplined, and proud—results don't have to be chased…they show up.

And to all the great employees who taught me along the way—

You taught me how to hire, train, replace, and promote—because the wrong person in the wrong seat will humble you fast, and the right person in the right seat will change everything. You gave me your talent, your effort, your patience, your pushback, and your pride in doing the job right. I owe you more than I can repay, and I carry deep gratitude for what you gave…even when it came with sleepless nights.

This book is my way of saying what I should've said more often: Thank you! If there's anything strong in these pages, it's because you stood with me, taught me, and helped shape what I could become. Any good that comes from this belongs to you—and any mistakes along the way were mine to learn.

Tim Whitt is an author-entrepreneur and operations-minded leader with 45 years of experience in the pest control industry—30 in corporate leadership and 15 building his own thriving company from the ground up. He founded Pied Piper Pest & Lawn in 2010 and grew it into a prevention-first, relationship-driven service brand serving Oklahoma and Texas. Known for disciplined execution and straightforward communication, the company maintains a 4.9-star reputation with 800+ customer reviews, with growth driven largely by referrals and a team culture built on accountability.

Whitt's writing comes from the field, not a seminar stage. After decades watching how problems spread—whether it's termites in a sill plate or drama in a break room—he developed a simple belief: behavior follows incentives, and incentives follow systems. That lens powers his book, *Infested: End Workplace Drama, Stop Toxic Employees, Build a Thriving Small Business*. In *Infested*, he uses pest behavior as a sharp, funny metaphor for people problems—employees, clients, and suppliers—so owners can stop reacting and start running a stable, profitable "business ecosystem."

Readers get practical tools to spot damaging behaviors early, set expectations without babysitting adults, and use lightweight data to make decisions instead of feeding the rumor mill. Whitt also tackles the hard parts most business books dodge: conflict that must be handled firmly, exits that must be done ethically, and standards that must be enforced consistently if you want calm operations and loyal teams. The tone is blunt but constructive—more "fix the root cause" than "post a motivational quote."

Based in southeastern Oklahoma, Tim lives with his best friend and wife of 44 years, Cindy—his steady partner through every season of business. When he's not writing, he's refining service delivery, training leaders, and helping owners build companies that don't depend on daily heroics. If something is chewing through morale, profit, or focus, Whitt's approach is simple: identify it, contain it, and eliminate it—then build safeguards so it doesn't come back.

www.ingramcontent.com/pod-product-compliance
Lightning Source LLC
Chambersburg PA
CBHW061519050726

47593CB00002B/646